John M. Smith

Memories of a First World War Sailor

Contents

Acknowledgements

Learning about the background of Uncle Johnnie's story has been more interesting and enjoyable than I could ever have imagined, and that is due mostly to the help that many folk have given me along the way. My thanks go out to all who have generously shared their time and their family history with me, or have inspired me in other ways. There are some that I must mention by name, and the first of those is Dave Smith, who agreed that I could publish our late, great Uncle Johnnie's story. He agreed that the proceeds should go to the RNLI, a charity long supported by our family. Later on, as the project neared completion, Dave skillfully improved the standard of many of the old family photographs. He also provided his lovely memories of Uncle Johnnie and researched key dates for the Smith (Moncrieff) family, providing the family tree in Appendix 3. For the Smith family photograph my thanks go to Janet Greenwood, granddaughter of George Smith. It's the only photograph that we have of Johnnie in uniform, possibly taken when he was home on leave sometime in 1915.

Early on in the project I was heartened and encouraged by the words, and assistance, of Linda Fitzpatrick, who is the Curator of the Scottish Fisheries Museum. I had met Linda a couple of years before, when donating old family items to the museum. As I wrote my first email to ask for her help I remember thinking that I was asking the impossible, but she gave me confidence with her enthusiastic reply, and I found the museum to be an excellent resource. Linda also put me in touch with others whose relatives had sailed with Uncle Johnnie, on the *Craignoon*, in the First World War.

Eilidh Lawrence generously sent me "all she had" about her relative Skipper James Brunton Wilson, along with his photograph taken at Anstruther Harbour. I am also indebted to Elizabeth Stormonth, whose grandfather John Corstorphine sailed briefly on the *Craignoon*, for her ability as a museum researcher. Elizabeth has been very supportive and made numerous trips to Anstruther library, discovering details of all kinds in the archives of local newspapers. There were some surprises in the "old news" which gave me new insight but also told of the chilling reality of those war time years and the dire situations folk found themselves in. Elizabeth and I also found that we are distant cousins; not too surprising in the East Neuk!

When previously researching local and family history, my late uncle, Sonny Corstorphine, had extensive knowledge and put me in touch with my "third cousin, once removed", Harry D. Watson. I am privileged to have had Harry's expert assistance and greatly value his *Kilrenny and Cellardyke: 800 Years of History* and his extensive knowledge of our family history. An author, translator and linguist, he was also editor and director of the Dictionary of the Older Scottish Tongue (DOST) at Edinburgh University. Harry told me that the completed DOST was now amalgamated in electronic format with the Scottish National Dictionary. It's possible to look up Scottish words from any period in time on their website, www.dsl.ac.uk. Harry has an absolute wealth of local knowledge and his detailed email replies invariably contained added entertainment! He knew my late mother, who also had a talent for, and a love of, writing. She was proud of her heritage and documented some of the old Cellardyke words and phrases to send to DOST.

I would like to thank Kevin Dunion for his generous consent to use material from his *Democracy of War*. I first contacted Kevin when writing a memorial leaflet for my late grandmother's brother, 'John Bett, Fisherman of Cellardyke', who died early in the First World War. Kevin collected information and photographs, family stories and even the inscriptions on the war memorials. He "tied them together" to provide a vivid and detailed picture of those war years 1914–1918 in Cellardyke and Anstruther. There must be many, like myself, who have discovered fascinating details which would otherwise have never been known.

We have many local books in our family collection and one of those, *Anstruther* by Stephanie Stevenson, provided the basis for the map showing the Craignoon coastal area, off John Street, Cellardyke. My thanks go to Jamie of Birlinn Ltd., publishers, for his quick response to my request for permission to copy and adapt the map. Another "thank you" goes to The Northern Lighthouse Board, which is the general lighthouse authority for Scotland. As a bit of a "long shot" I sent them a photograph to identify the location. They kindly circulated it and "Tubby" spotted that it was taken at Gorleston, Yarmouth. At the same time, my second cousin, Bob Smith, confirmed the identification as Yarmouth. I wanted to use this family photograph as I find it fascinating; it gives a feeling of the urgency and excitement of the steam drifters juggling themselves in towards the port, loaded with their catches of herring.

My heartfelt and grateful thanks go to my close cousin, James K. Corstorphine, who has long been interested in preserving local knowledge of the history of the East Neuk, and the old Scottish Dialect particular to the area. Jimmy responded warmly and generously to my many requests for information and readily gave his permission for the use of any material from the books he has published. He also gave me copies of the Peter Smith books.

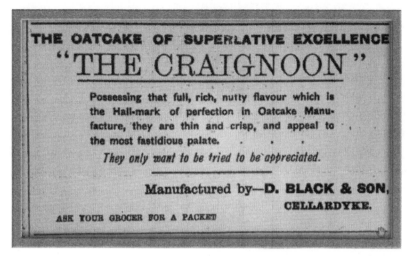

An advertisement for an oatcake sharing the name of Johnnie's wartime drifter, published in the 8th June 1916 edition of the East Fife Record, and rediscovered by Elizabeth Stormonth.

It would take many paragraphs to thank my daughter, Meg Humphries, properly! Whilst we agreed that we would leave Johnnie's story un-edited, Meg's expertise in writing was reassuring and this gave me confidence, especially with my research notes. Her knowledge of proofreading and copy-editing (through her business www.greenstarproofreading.co.uk) meant that it was possible to concentrate on the content, with the knowledge that she would keep an eye on not only spelling, grammar and punctuation but would also make sure that it all made sense. When it came to publishing, Meg had an abundance of information and, most importantly, she found ways to make sure that all was financially viable. It made all the difference, and I must say that I could not have completed this project without her help. Thank you, Meg. It has been a real pleasure to work with you.

This has certainly been a family affair, so, last but not least, I must thank my husband Tim – who has been most patient whilst waiting to "grab a slot" on the PC and has cooked many a meal for us whilst I was busy! But more than that, he is always kind and supportive – and has many talents, not least helping me with a little bit of research, especially finding online resources in the early days and pointing me in the right direction.

Research about one thing often leads to even more intrigue and unanswered questions than before and, as such, my research is ongoing and potentially lifelong! I therefore welcome any other useful information related to topics in this book, and I can be contacted at ali_humphries@outlook.com.

This story is being published to thank, commemorate and celebrate all those ordinary people, the "brave and cheerful" folk – the men and the women – in the past and in the present time, especially those whose work takes them onto the sea.

Alison Humphries (née Kingscott), 2017

Uncle Johnnie

"Uncle" Johnnie was not actually my uncle but was in fact my dad's uncle. He was the nearest my brother Robert and I had to a grandfather. He was small and rotund with a very jolly face and had a great sense of humour, some of it quite lavatorial. Enough said.

In my late primary school years and early teens we used to go by car from Cellardyke to Burntisland for our summer holidays and stayed with Uncle Johnnie and his wife Nellie. This seemed like a great adventure, but the distance was actually less than 30 miles.

While we stayed there, Uncle Johnnie would come home on many occasions with a big beaming smile on his face and announce that he had bought some "slimming" cakes. They were, of course, not "slimming" cakes as they usually had thick icing on top or thick cream inside and sometimes had both! There would be a great amount of chuckling from him, which was very infectious to us young boys.

My other vivid memory of him was of him smoking his pipe. He used to scrape at the bowl of the pipe with his penknife. There was then much tapping to remove all the burnt tobacco. The bowl was filled with fresh tobacco and was firmed down with the match box. It was lit and after about half a dozen puffs the pipe invariably went out. The whole procedure would start all over again.

He would recall some of his stories as a POW in the First World

War and was especially proud of the amount of times that he managed to escape. Again much chuckling!

He frequently had a mischievous twinkle in his eyes and would suddenly burst into song with a little ditty that he had just made up. This would result in him getting a scolding from Nellie. His head would shrink down into his shoulders and then his infectious chuckle would begin.

These are my wonderful memories of this lovely, fun-filled and very kindly man, Uncle Johnnie.

Dave Smith

Uncle Johnnie (top left) and David (bottom right) with Nellie and David Smith Senior.

1

We are Prisoners on an Enemy Ship

When we left Anstruther in the steam drifter *Craignoon* to go to Aberdeen to be under the Navy patrol, we only had a skeleton crew – James Wilson, skipper, of Cellardyke; David Dunn, mate, of Pittenweem; Tom Duff, 1st engineer from Alloa; myself, the 2nd engineer from Anstruther; WilliamMcKenzie, deckhand, of Pittenweem, and John Corstorphine, another deckhand, from Cellardyke.

On arrival at Aberdeen we were all issued with uniforms and got our crew made up with Glasgow and Aberdeen men. Then we had orders to proceed to Falmouth in Cornwall – getting "bunkers" at an English port on our way south.

When we arrived at Falmouth we found a few drifters there before us. The first drifter to arrive there was the Anstruther boat *Dreel Castle*, so they named the base H.M.S. *Dreel Castle*. We had a fine time there patrolling between Lizard Head and Penzance, and sometimes to the east of Falmouth, in St. Austell Bay between Dodman Point and Looe.

One day the mate and I had orders to fill up with coal, to prepare for going out to Gibraltar. When the coaling started the two Glasgow crewmen slipped ashore and left the mate and myself with the trimming of the coal into the bunkers. But the coalmen were coming so fast with the bags that we could not cope with them, so we had to give up.

When the 1st engineer came back from leave I reported to him what had happened, and that we would not have enough coal to take us to Gibraltar. He said: "Well, the other boats will have to tow us."

We left Falmouth the next day with 20 other drifters for Gibraltar. The weather was fine, with just a bit of swell on the water. When we were half way across the Bay of Biscay, however, we ran up a signal to the flagship that we were short of coal. The flagship then went round the fleet and ordered them all to put out all the lumps of coal they could spare on their decks and take their turn to steam slowly past us and throw the coal on to our deck.

So that is how we got "bunkers" in the middle of the Bay of Biscay – to enable us to carry on with the fleet to Gibraltar.

After two days in Gibraltar getting in stores, water and coal, we sailed out into the Mediterranean, heading for Italy.

For over eight days and nights we did four hours' duty on and four hours' duty off, and the heat in the engineroom was terrific. We could not hold on to the iron ladder leading to the deck too long or we would have burned our hands.

At last we arrived in Brindisi on the south-east coast of Italy – which was to be our base for a year or so.

One day our group of drifters had orders to patrol off the coast of Durazzo in Albania, and when we got there we found the sea was a mass of wreckage, and dead cattle and mines floating all around. We were there for a few hours and destroyed many mines. The flagship then gave us the signal to proceed in single line back to Brindisi. When it became dark we all slowed down as we could not enter Brindisi until daylight.

I was on watch in the engineroom and had a peep out of the skylight for a breath of air when I noticed we were nearly up alongside the flagship, so I jumped down and put the engine down dead slow. Ten minutes later I had another look and saw the flagship just ahead of us.

I was just back in the engineroom about five minutes when there was a big explosion ahead of us, and I was told to stop the engines. Some time later we learned that the flagship had struck a mine and there was no sign of any survivors. When daylight came we searched among the wreckage but there was no sign of any of the crew, so we just had to get underway again and sail back to our base in Brindisi.

One day one of our crew, William McKenzie of Pittenweem, put in for promotion to 2nd engineer and within a few days was sent for and made 2nd engineer on the Fraserburgh drifter *Morning Star*. All of us on the *Craignoon* thought a lot of McKenzie and were pleased at his promotion.

The next day the *Morning Star* went to sea with her group and a few hours later news came to the base that she had struck a mine and there were no survivors. We were all grieved to hear the sad news, for McKenzie had been with us a long time and it was like losing a brother.

A few months later our base was transferred to Taranto in the Gulf of Taranto.

When we were out in the Straits of Otranto fishing for submarines with the steel wire nets, the Austrian destroyers frequently made raids on the line of drifters – very often in the dark.

One quiet, dark night heavy gunfire started not far from where we were lying at the nets, so we let them go and steamed towards the firing. When we got there the destroyers had gone and nothing but wreckage was left of one of our group – the Fraserburgh drifter *Beneficient*. There were no survivors and I lost a good shore chum in the drifter's 2nd engineer.

Another day we were returning to our base with our group after a spell at sea when our skipper spotted a floating mine, well to our starboard side, so he altered course and headed for it. Our custom was to fire a sixpound shell from our 50mm Italian gun, which made a hole in the mine, causing it to sink to the bottom. We went rather too close to this mine – then fired.

The shot struck one of the plungers and it blew up. At the same time the engineroom telegraph rang – "Full speed astern" – and I, being on watch, gave her the lot. I wondered at the time if the bow had been blown off.

The rest of the group heard the explosion and saw the smoke over us and thought we'd had it. But we came out of it all right, without any casualties. I picked up a piece of the mine in the stokehold which had come through the vent. We thought then that our turn was sure to come.

And come it did – on May 15th 1917, a date I will remember more than any other. Our position in the line was about five or six miles west of Faro Island, on the Albanian side of the Adriatic, and at 4 am I was roused with the half of the crew who were off watch and told to get on deck as there was heavy gunfire to the west of us.

We could make out two big ships firing heavy guns. Then, when daylight broke, we saw an enemy cruiser coming up from the south. He came up on the east side of our group and I saw a gun crew on one drifter running to their gun. The next moment a shot from the cruiser hit the gun and the gun crew.

The rest of us had no escape. We had two enemy cruisers on the west side of us and one on the east and our small gun was no match against armed cruisers.

I kicked off my boots in case I had to take to the water and said to the skipper, "Well, what is it to be?"

He said, "Tell the 1st engineer to stop the engine and come up on deck and get the small boat over."

We all got into the small boat (the skipper coming aboard last) and immediately a shot rang out and bang went the wheelhouse! We pulled away from the drifter as fast as we could. The second shell must have hit the boiler with high steam pressure on for our ship blew up in pieces from the forehold to the stern. The stem of the forehold floated for a minute, then fell over and sank.

It was a good thing the weather was calm that morning for with all the crew being in the drifter's small boat she was sitting very low in the water.

The shells were still flying – sinking other drifters – so we had to keep low in the small boat. We saw another three crews in their small boats so we pulled up beside them.

After the cruiser *Novara* (which had sunk our drifter) had finished sinking the others, she came after us in the small boats.

When I saw the bow of the cruiser coming towards us I thought he was going to ram us; then I saw the splashing of the propellers and knew he was going full astern. An officer from the bridge shouted, "Come aboard, please," and when we moved alongside, we saw many ropes hanging from the side of the ship. I caught hold of one of the ropes and started climbing and the Austrian sailors pulled on the other end. Soon I was on the deck of the cruiser.

All the other crews were pulled up in the same way and we were sent down to the second deck below the bridge.

Then one of the Austrian sailors brought down hot tea (mixed with some sort of sweet wine) and some black bread. They also gave us some cigarettes for which we were very thankful. On the whole we were very well treated all the time we were on the cruiser.

2

Our Starvation Ordeal at Enemy Hands

About 8 am the alarm bell went and the guns started again. But it did not last long. We asked the Austrian sailor who was keeping guard over us (and who spoke good English) what it was, and he said it was Italian aircraft and two French destroyers. He smiled and said one of the destroyers was in difficulties.

About 9 am the alarm went again. We were told it was three British cruisers this time, and the crew seemed to be more excited than worried. Five minutes later both sides went into action.

The three British cruisers were the *Liverpool*, *Dartmouth* and *Bristol*. Where we were we could see nothing, only hear the reports of the guns from both sides.

The shells from the British cruisers were exploding on the ship we were on and we could hear the cries of the wounded and dying men.

It was a trying position for us to be in for every minute we expected a shell to come through to us, and, if that had happened, we would have been caught like rats in a trap.

The fight went on… the Austrians working their way north to their base at Cattaro all the time. The cruiser we were on got a terrible battering and at 2 pm the engine slowed down and stopped; we could tell this from the change in the vibration of the ship. We were now a sitting target for the British ships and we could do nothing but still hope for the best.

Then there was a crash and our ship started to list, so we all jumped to our feet. Our Austrian guard told us it was all right – that one of their own cruisers had come alongside to tow us as the engineroom was out of action. While we were being towed (about five miles an hour) the fight was at its hottest. We kept wondering how much longer the *Novara* could hold out. The British cruisers had the upper hand (as the Austrian sailor admitted later) and my companions and I expected we would soon be in Davy Jones's locker with the *Novara*.

But just at that moment one of Austria's latest type of battleships came out of Cattaro and chased the British ships. Then the gunfire stopped. It was now 4 pm. As far as the Austrians were concerned the battle was over. The casualties on board the *Novara* were 15 killed and 25 wounded. The commander was killed and the captain was injured.

When we arrived in Cattaro (about 7 pm after having been towed all the way by the cruiser *Heligoland*) there was a great deal of cheering. When it was nearly dark we were all taken up on deck to be taken ashore.

But we could not go along the port side of the deck as is was a mass of wreckage. The bridge and funnels were also smashed. We were taken ashore in launches.

When we arrived at the jetty there were two lines of Austrian soldiers and we had to march in between these two lines. All the clothes I had on consisted of navy overalls and I was in my bare feet, having kicked off my shoes and socks when the shelling of our drifter started that morning.

We were marched up a stony hill road for about an hour and a half to an old Montenegrin fortress with cobbled stones inside the yard. The officer in charge led us to an open shed with straw spread out over the cobbled stones. This was to be our bed for the night!

I remember walking over to the shed, my feet cut and sore, but I don't remember lying down. I must have dropped unconscious immediately. Later I was told that it was 1 am when we had arrived at the fortress, so it had been a long and trying day for us all – from 4 am the day before, when the shelling of our drifter fleet had started.

That morning we were handed a ladleful of coffee for our breakfast – but nothing to eat. We met other drifter crews who had had their ships sunk by the cruisers *Heligoland* and *Saida*. There were 72 of us altogether.

The 1st and 2nd enginemen of the Buckie drifter *Quarry Knowe* had been killed. She was hit several times – one shell going through the engineroom, killing the 2nd engineer and wounding the 1st. The latter managed to get up on deck and into the small boat. He was then taken on board the Austrian cruiser, where he died two hours later. He was taken ashore at Cattaro and buried, as were the Austrian sailors who had been killed that day.

At 11 am on the first day in the fortress we were each given a piece of bread (made from maize) about the size of three or four fingers. Half an hour later we received a ladleful of sauerkraut (it looked like sliced cabbage, cured in barrels with some kind of sour liquid – probably vinegar). We could not eat it and dumped it in a heap in a corner.

But we were in for a shock. Our Austrian guards went over and picked up the sour cabbage we had thrown away and ate it themselves!

That was all the food we got each day, so we had to eat it. We picked out any maggots we saw – and got it down. Austria was in a terrible state of starvation and could not spare us any more food.

After being in this fortress for four days we were all marched down to the town to get a shower-bath (of cold water) and a haircut which made us all look like convicts. Our clothes were fumigated, then we marched back to the fortress.

The next day those who hadn't much clothing were issued with some. I received an old white cotton shirt, a pair of soldier's old boots (the top half of them canvas), two strips of white cotton cloth to wrap round my feet for socks, a pair of brown corduroy trousers and a brown corduroy jumper, the same style as a fisherman's jumper.

But I had to hand over my good flannel shirt and my suit of overalls, which were warmer than the things I had just received. We looked a funny lot indeed with all these different clothes on.

The next day, the 21st May, at 4.30 am, we were all marched to the station. We were put into cattle trucks, but the skippers went into proper carriages. We were being taken to a prison in a town called Graz. We were three days and nights travelling to Graz. The cattle truck I was in held 30 men and the two guards sat in the middle – one on each side – beside the sliding doors. These were kept open about a foot to let the air in.

The nights were very cold travelling through the mountainous part of Yugoslavia and we all suffered from the cold and starvation. We stopped each day, about midday, to get our usual bowl of sauerkraut and a piece of bread. One day we stopped at a soldiers' camp and we received a bowl of potato soup – which tasted so good after the monotony of daily sauerkraut.

One man got a bone with a piece of gristle on it and he threw it away. Two Russian soldiers then made a dive for it and had a fight over it.

When we arrived at Graz on the 24th May we were put on motor lorries and rushed through the town to a quarantine prison. This prison was in the middle of the town – a huge building with iron bars on all the windows. There were no beds so we just had to stretch out on the floor, with a certain number of men to each room. There was the usual starvation diet, so we were all getting weaker every day.

3

Two Tins of Meat our Key to Freedom

After 25 days in this prison we were marched out and told we were going to a camp, but, instead of driving us to the station in the lorries, we had to march. We could now see that the Austrians were going to make us a "showpiece" for the people of Graz, to give them the impression that Britain was starving and in a bad way – not knowing that we had been starved in their own town.

The officer in charge took us through all the main streets, and the people there just stared at us. Some asked the guards what nationality we were and were told that we were "Englanders". We were a pitiful sight and were hardly able to do that hour's walk to the station.

Then, all at once, some of the men started singing "It's a long way to Tipperary", and other wartime songs followed. This seemed to put new life into us and the singing was good from 70 voices.

We arrived at the station and were bundled into cattle trucks again – and the skippers with us this time. 25 to 30 men in each truck and we left immediately for a prisoner-of-war camp – destination unknown. On 21st June we arrived at a small town called Deutsch Gabel, in Bohemia – about three miles from the German border. (That part of Europe is now called Czechoslovakia.)

After we got out of the trucks we were marched to the POW camp – about a quarter of an hour's walk away. When we got into the camp we were taken into a long army hut with wooden bunks, straw mattresses and a straw pillow, but this was heaven compared to how we'd had to rough it for the last five weeks.

This camp at Deutsch Gabel was a fine, healthy place and we met another drifter's crew there who had been taken prisoner nine months previous. There were also four French submarine crews and about two thousand Russian soldiers. After we were settled down in this camp – with plenty of room to walk about and plenty of good fresh air for a change – I met another two East Fife men from other drifters – George Watson of Cellardyke and James Aitken of St. Monance.

We were still getting the same starvation diet at this camp – a drink of coffee or green tea in the morning, without sugar or milk, and a small piece of bread with a ladleful of sauerkraut (sometimes we got potato soup) at midday – that was our whole day's rations. There was a canteen in the camp but all we could get there was needles and thread, buttons, or smoking pipes – no tobacco, or anything to eat.

I bought one of the German pipes and acquiring some green tea leaves from the cooks in the kitchen I dried them in the sun and used them for tobacco. It was a rough smoke but it helped to ease the pangs of hunger.

We had a very weary time waiting for letters from home – it was nearly three months before we got any. We were all very weak for want of food and could not walk far without having a rest. Starvation is a very cruel thing – it is like something inside you eating at your body all the time. You can see your ribs sticking out and all the bones in your hand showing.

We were allowed to write a letter home and a Red Cross card on

13

alternate weeks. After we had been in the camp for about three months we began to get Red Cross parcels of food, sent from the Navy League Committee, London, and oh, didn't we enjoy that first feed! In some of the parcels there was a tin of "bully beef", box of portion cheese, packets of porridge oats, packets of biscuits and many other foods.

After the first consignment of parcels arrived we got them pretty regularly and we also received cigarettes and tobacco!

As the weeks went by our health and strength improved, and we were now able to walk right round the camp enjoying our smoke of real tobacco!

The French sailors received a football, and they asked our men to make up two teams. I was made a left half-back in our second team and we played quite a few games with them. In one of the games – played against the French second team – I rushed to meet one of them coming up my wing with the ball, and when he was about two yards away he kicked the ball with force. It struck me on the face and knocked me flat on my back. That finished me with football!

It wasn't long before each man received a parcel of clothing. A new uniform, underclothes, boots, and a heavy overcoat. These were sent from London and we felt like new persons after that.

The Austrians now saw we were able-bodied men and they decided to send us to another camp – to work. So we got orders to leave the following day – all except the skippers and the first enginemen. They were to stay on at Deutsch Gabel.

Next day we travelled to a prison camp at Laibach (this time in proper carriages – not cattle trucks as before). I did not like the camp at Laibach. The hut we were put in was small, not too clean, and it did not look a healthy camp. There were a few thousand Russians in it and quite a lot of Italians.

We soon found it was a stone-breaking camp we had been sent to. Our men were made into four or five groups with a petty officer in charge of each group. There were about 15 petty officers (including mates and enginemen) so we had to draw lots to see who was in charge of each group.

I was one of the lucky ones. All I had to do was to march the men off in the morning to the stone-breaking quarry. I was in the lead with one of the Austrian guards, and, once there, I sat down and had a smoke of my pipe, while the men were breaking the stones. This went on day after day.

Often when we were marching out of the camp we would see parties of big (six-foot) Russian soldiers, hardly able to walk, and eating the grass at the roadside. It was pitiful to see them, and it was a common thing for some of them to drop dead of starvation. They did not get any food parcels as we did.

I was getting sick of seeing so much suffering, and having to stay in this unhealthy camp, so I decided I would escape from it. I handed over my job as supervisor of the group to an older man who was working in another group, and I took his place for a few days. My new job was to feed a stone-crusher. The stones were round and they sometimes went flying out of the crusher and up into the air to a height of perhaps twenty feet. You had to jump for your life if that happened for you knew these stones had to come down again!

Well, three of us arranged to escape. James Ross from Aberdeen, a 2nd engineman (cannot remember his name) also from Aberdeen, and myself. We bribed an old Austrian guard with three tins of meat, to let us through the wire fence at a certain corner. At the last minute the 2nd engineman backed out, so we cancelled it for the time being.

The next day James Ross came to me and said, "Here's an

Italian sergeant who has been a POW since the beginning of the war, and is now a trusted prisoner; he has a pass to take one or two prisoners of war for a walk. (He speaks good German and English.) He said he would take us out – for two tins of beef!"

So, next day, at dinner-time, when things were quietest, James Ross and I marched towards the gate with the Italian sergeant – with our haversacks on our backs. We had biscuits and tinned food, and I had my Russian water bottle filled to the brim. When we came to the gate the Italian showed the guard his pass, and told him we were going out to the farms to get flour in exchange for tinned food, and the guard let us pass.

The Italian said we were not clear yet as we walked along the country road; he said there were Austrian patrols at different places for about a mile from the camp. When we came near a brickwork or quarry building, two Austrian soldiers stepped out and told us to halt. The Italian handed the pass and told him the same story. He looked at us (we gave him a smile!) and he let us carry on with our journey.

We walked on for another half-hour, then we came to a forest. Our friend said we were clear now and bade us good-bye and good luck. He told us he would have to take another road back and go into the camp by another gate.

So James Ross and I started off on our own – on our first leap to freedom.

4

Our Flight by Train and Foot

We marched through the edge of the forest till it was nearly dark, then lay down beside a big tree and fell asleep. We slept until morning and for our breakfast we had a slice of raw Ayrshire bacon (the bacon we received in one of our Red Cross parcels) and two tea biscuits – washed down with water.

We could have eaten more but had to ration ourselves as the Red Cross parcels would likely stop for us now that we weren't at the camp.

Before we escaped we bought a small compass (the size of an old-fashioned watch) and a map of Austria from a Russian soldier – for a few biscuits. Our plan was to get down to the Adriatic coast, near Trieste, and "pinch" a small boat in the dark, in an attempt to get across to the Italian coast. So we studied the map and the compass showed us the course to take. We scanned the land on our course and we saw a hill in the distance, so we headed for that – walking always in daylight.

When we came to the hill we had a look at the compass again and took another landmark. Sometimes it was a church steeple (if we were near a village) and sometimes it was a farm. About noon each day we would sit down at the side of the road and open a tin of beef between us, and eat that with a slice of raw turnip (which we pinched from a field), or a slice of raw potato, and we washed it down with "Adam's wine" from our flask.

We always managed to get our water flasks filled from the burns or rivers. For tea we had two tea biscuits, with a small portion of cheese and for supper we put a handful of porridge oats into our enamel bowls, added some cold water, gave it a stir and got it down!

We always tried to get near forests or bits of woodland at night-time as we were sheltered from the wind, and we always slept soundly beneath the trees after our supper of cold porridge oats.

On the third morning on the run we woke up in the forest and had our usual light breakfast. Then we made for the main road again.

We had to wade through thick undergrowth of young trees and long grass – and I stepped on a wasps' nest! We were stung all over our necks, faces and hands. We ran – stumbling and falling – till we reached the main road, to get room to knock them off us and kill them. We suffered plenty that day with blisters all over our faces and necks, but in time we found a brook and we had a good wash, which helped to cool our stinging faces.

About 5 pm on our fifth day, the sky got very black, so I suggested to my mate that we should head for a farm about half a mile away, as it would be too wet for sleeping out. When we got near the farm we kept the barns between us and the farm in case we were spotted from the house. When we got about a hundred yards from the barn, down came the rain with thunder and lightning for good measure. So we made a dash into a big shed for holding farm machinery.

When we got inside we noticed a lot of planks of wood up in the rafters, so we climbed up, spread out some of the planks and lay down for the night. The rain was lashing down outside, but we were soon fast asleep.

In the morning we were wakened by a noise below us. I looked down and saw the farmer and a farm worker taking out some farm tools, so we kept very quiet until they were well out of sight. Then we had a snack of two biscuits and slice of bacon, washed down again with simple water, slipped out and were off on the road again.

This was the sixth day on the run. At about 11 am we came to a small one-sided railway station and, as our feet were getting pretty sore from all the walking, Ross went boldly into the station and asked the two booking clerks when we would get a train for Trieste. He was told 12 noon. So we decided to risk travelling by rail as we both had money sent from home and had had it changed into Austrian currency.

About 11.15 am a goods train with empty wagons came into the station and the engine started taking in water for the boiler. I told Ross, "Let's take a walk round the end of the trucks and we might get the chance of a free ride in one of them."

When we got round the other side of the trucks we noticed one wagon with the door down and, as it was open country on this side, we thought it quite safe to jump into the wagon as the train was moving off. We were just settling down when a head appeared at the other side, shouting something in German! We didn't waste a second. We both jumped off and ran at the double across the country!

After we were well clear of that station we decided to walk to the next one and catch the noon train there. We did not have long to wait and when the train came in we went abroad and thankfully sat down.

It soon pushed off and as Ross was better at speaking German than I was I gave him all the money I had and told him to do all the talking and pay for the tickets. We were on the train about an hour when the ticket collector came round so Ross asked him for two single tickets to Trieste. He wrote out one ticket for both of us, but when he counted our money he said we didn't have enough to go to Trieste so he altered the town name on our ticket and we sat back quite pleased with ourselves.

After we had travelled a few hours on that train we had to get out at a big station to change. We were walking quietly about the station when a big gendarme came up to us. He asked where we were going and Ross said: "To work on a farm." He then asked too many questions in German and Ross could not answer them all.

So the gendarme said: "Come," and we were led away to the guard-room at the station. We slept on the guardroom floor that night and when we awakened in the morning we found our map and compass gone. They had been through our pockets while we slept. If we had been able to speak German properly I believe we could have made a success of our escape.

We wore a blue uniform and navy overcoat, with civilian buttons, and a peak cap without a badge.

A policeman gave us coffee then Austrian soldiers came and escorted us to a camp about half an hour's walk away. When we arrived at the camp we were taken into an office to be questioned by the general. He asked if we were English and we said we were (I nearly said, "No, we're Scots!") He spoke very good English and asked what camp we escaped from. We did not want to go back to the stone-breaking camp in Laibach so we said we escaped from Deutsch Gabel in Bohemia – the camp we went to in the first place.

He would not believe this as it was such a long journey, and said: "How did you travel from there?" I told him partly by train and partly walking. He still would not believe it, so I showed him an old letter from my mother with my name, number, and "Deutsch Gabel" addressed on the envelope. He believed us then.

He then told us to turn out our haversacks so he could see what we were carrying. He was amazed when he saw the contents – tea, biscuits, bully beef, cheese, porridge oats, a cut of bacon, a tin of herring and tinned stew. I told him we had got these in our Red Cross parcels sent from London. He said: "I never see as much food as that and I am a general." He then told us that he would have to put us in the cells for a few days, till arrangements could be made to send us back to Deutsch Gabel.

We were put in separate cells but we could see each other through holes in the wooden wall between us. The cells were about ten feet long, and four feet wide. A guard walked to and fro in the passage outside. We were given a bucket of water each and I could see a Russian soldier on the other side of me – through holes in the opposite wall. The next day we received the usual sauerkraut, a small piece of maize bread, and a raw salt herring! I kept the piece of bread for my tea and got the sauerkraut down.

Then I had a peep at the Russian. He was eating his raw salt herring so I thought, if it doesn't kill him it won't kill me, and I started on mine. I got head, tail, bones (the lot) down, and followed it with a huge drink of water, I then stretched out on the floor quite content.

5

Punishment Cells – But it's Not So Bad

On the fourth day in the cells, we were taken out and told we were going back to Deutsch Gabel. Two guards marched us to the station and all four of us went into one carriage, the guards keeping watch at each doorway.

It was a long journey back and when we arrived my old skipper, James Wilson, gave me a bowl of warm porridge oats, which I enjoyed immensely. I was put into a cell, but James Ross, who had become ill as a result of the rough handling we had, was taken to hospital.

After one night in the cell, I was taken before the general. He could not speak English, so all conversation was through a Russian interpreter. He asked why I had escaped and I told him it was my duty to try and escape.

I told him it was against the rules of war to make me work on stone-breaking as I was a petty officer. The answer I got, through the interpreter, was: "We are short of men and you will have to work. It is also my duty to punish you." The punishment was 15 days in the cells.

After my 15 days were up I had one night in the camp, then, in the morning, a guard came and took me up to the gate – where I saw two English, who had been taken prisoners on the Italian front. I was told that all three were being sent to Laibach – the stone-breaking camp I had escaped from earlier. I still had some of the Red Cross parcel food in my haversack so I was determined I wasn't going to give in yet.

On the road to the station I said to the English soldiers: "When we get to Reichenberg we will have to change trains, so while we are waiting on the platform I want you to speak to the guards, point to church steeples or anything to draw their attention away from me, as I mean to escape." This happened and I got my chance to escape; mingling with the crowd I soon got out of the station. When I came to the ticket collector at the gate I just waved my hand and carried on walking.

After I had been away about two hours I came near the outskirts of the town, so I carried on along the country road. Suddenly a gendarme came out from behind a hedge asked me where I was going. I told him I was on my way to work. But he had me beat when he began to ask me some more questions in German! So he said, "Come!" and I was marched away once more! He took me to a camp near at hand and I was taken before an officer who spoke good English.

He asked me if I was English and I said I was; but I didn't answer truthfully to all his other questions. "Now, now," he said. "You're not telling me the truth."

So I told him I had escaped from the guards at the station because they were taking me to a stone-breaking camp and I had never done that sort of work.

I also told him I was a petty officer and should not be working. He said I should have told the general that at Deutsch Gabel. I said I had told him but it made no difference.

He said he would put me in the cells for a few days, then send me back to Deutsch Gabel. I was then marched off with an Austrian sergeant to a brand new camp about a mile away. The camp was empty. He put me in a cell and handed me a bucket of water. He went away, and for three days I was in that cell, in an empty camp, and nobody came near me. I had some food in my haversack but I knew it would not last me forever. I thought if nobody came the next day I would smash at the wooden door and get out.

But, about 8 am on the fourth morning I heard footsteps, then a key turning in the lock, and the Austrian sergeant came in. He said, "Come – Deutsch Gabel!"

He took me back to the station I had escaped from, and went with me by train to Deutsch Gabel. When I arrived again at the camp the skippers were surprised but pleased to see me again. I had to spend the night in a cell and go before the general in the morning.

He spoke to me again through the interpreter, asking me why I had escaped. I said not to get out of the country this time, but because I was being sent to the stone-breaking camp. I was determined not to give in. Then he had his say: 15 days in cells and six hours each day in irons.

Then the sergeant took me (once more) to the cells. He opened his box of shackles with the chains and tied one on my arm. It was a fine size, but I made out it was too tight, so he gave me a bigger size.

It was quite slack on my arm, but I told him "Good" and he locked it on my right arm with the other end on my left ankle. There was only about a foot of chain between my wrist and ankle, and I was to sit for six hours each day in this cramped position. The sergeant said he didn't like doing this but he had to obey orders.

After he went away I wet my hand and slipped the shackle of, and stretched full out on the floor. The guard came running along the passage and looked through the peep-hole in the door. He had obviously heard the chain rattle to the floor and rushed in with a rifle in his hand, shouting, "Report, report!" I gave him an English cigarette and said: "Nein report?" (meaning "no report") and he agreed.

After the 15 days were up I was taken into the camp and told I was being sent to an officers' camp near Vienna – to be an officers' orderly – the next morning.

When I was ready to go I met another two English soldiers who were going there too as orderlies. A Dundee skipper came to see us off, and he said to me: "Will you be back again?" I said I would see what the camp was like – if it was good I would stay, but if it wasn't, I would be back in Deutsch Gabel – to do more time!

Two Austrian guards came to take us on our journey. Just then the Dundee skipper recognised one of them to be one of the guards I had escaped from at Reichenberg station and mentioned it to him. The guard then recognised me. He told me that he had got into serious trouble for letting me escape. We then marched to the station and boarded the train. Again we had to change at Reichenberg, so, while we were waiting on the platform, I said to one of the guards that I was going for a drink of water, and walked away. When I got to the station water-tap he was right at my back! The guard was right on my heels all the time – just to make sure I could not escape from him this time.

At last we arrived at the officers' camp – not far from Vienna. There were no wooden huts there, all stone buildings, about five or six storeys high. Two English soldiers and myself had a room on the ground floor, with three iron beds in it. The following day I was taken upstairs to meet an Aberdeen Air Force captain, and was told I was to be his orderly. Then I met an Edinburgh lieutenant. I was to be his orderly too. All I had to do was to shake their army blankets and make their beds, and sweep the floors if they needed sweeping. About 15 minutes' work for each officer – plenty for an unpaid servant.

This was a good, clean, healthy camp and I would have been happy here if I had had more food – and a smoke. My Red Cross food was finished and I was now on the Austrian starvation diet. I did not expect any more parcels, and my tobacco was also finished.

One morning, when I went to make the captain's bed, he went out for a walk, and, after doing my usual chores, I noticed a good-sized tin on his table. I lifted the lid and peered in, and behold, it was three-quarters filled with tobacco mixture! He had received it in a private parcel from home. (A commissioned officer was allowed to get private parcels from home, but lower ranks weren't allowed that privilege.) Well, I yielded to temptation and took a handful of tobacco out.

Then I shook the rest of the tobacco up till it looked almost three-quarters full again. I went for a walk and had a good smoke with my German pipe. That eased the awful pangs of hunger for a time. (If that captain happens to read this, I will give him a full tin of tobacco for what I pinched from him that day.)

6

Forbidden Fruit in the Garden of Eden

Prisoners of good behaviour were allowed outside the camp for a walk at times (with a guard). So my turn came one afternoon – but that was the only turn I got. There were two of us and a guard and as we walked along the road I noticed Victoria plums growing on trees by the side of the road.

I drew the guard's attention to this, and pointed to them but he shouted, "Nein. Nein!"

I said "Yah. Yah," and grabbed two big juicy plums and handed them to him because he was just as hungry as we were – but he did not want to do the stealing.

I jumped up again and pulled half a dozen for myself, and that eased the hunger for that day. But I did not get another chance to go into the "Garden of Eden" – with the "forbidden fruit".

One day I was putting some rubbish in the bin when I saw a whole loaf of English bread in it. It must have been put there by an officer who had received it in a private parcel. I lifted it out and saw it was mouldy but I thought I might clean it up and make some good food from it, so I took it to my room.

I asked the two English soldiers to bring their enamel bowls as I intended to make "bread saps" with it. I cut out the black bits and broke up the rest into the three bowls. I added water and stirred the mixture till it was soft and swollen and we had a feed of "saps".

Our hunger was satisfied but through the night we suffered with pains in the tummy. In the morning we drank a lot of water and the pains eventually stopped.

One afternoon the three of us were called out by an officer to empty a motor wagon filled with boxes of biscuits. The boxes were wooden, about three feet long, and a foot and a half wide. They were to be stored in an empty room on the top floor of the building in case of emergency (I think they had come from Switzerland).

I carried the first box up the long winding stone stair and handed it to the officer who was counting the boxes as they came in.

On the way down I thought of us being on a starvation diet, and having to carry all these biscuits to be stored in an empty room – so I thought I would do a bit of plotting.

When I was carrying up the second box I dropped it and the box burst open. I filled all my pockets with biscuits and when I reached the top floor I told the officer that the box had burst but he just said to put it beside the rest. I rushed down to my room, emptied my pockets and ran to the wagon for the next box.

I gave the hint to my two team-mates what to do to ward off starvation. The third box I didn't hit so hard on the steps and only one board was loosened but again I managed to fill my pockets. Then I put the board back into place and carried up the box.

We had to do things like this to survive and to keep the bones in our hands and chests from sticking out too far. I now had a good stock of biscuits and I knew if I economised they would last me quite a while.

Well the happy day came at last. We were all called to the middle of the camp (officers and men) to hear what the Austrian commanding officer had to say. He told us that Austria was finished with the war and he was withdrawing all the guards from the camp. He told us we were free to walk about as we wished but if we waited for two days he would arrange to get a special train to take us to the seaport at Trieste.

Before we left, the British officer in charge of the biscuits told us to go upstairs and take as many as we could carry as we might not get any Austrian food on our journey to Trieste. I filled up my haversack and all my pockets, and I reckoned this would last me till I reached England. There were plenty of biscuits left so the hungry Austrians would get their share.

The day came when we were all assembled to march to the station. I had filled my Russian water flask and was very happy that I had plenty of biscuits and water to tide me over on my journey.

Travelling to Trieste by rail we saw many trains going in the opposite direction. They were full of Austrian soldiers coming from the front – a good many hanging on to the outside of the carriages.

When we reached Trieste we were put on board an old cargo boat which took us across the upper reaches of the Adriatic Sea and landed us in Venice. The Italians put us in a big house and kept us in quarantine for six days. We were all glad to get out of there and on to the train to France.

We had to change at a station near the border and after a short time a train came in. I heard one man say, "This is our train," and he rushed into a carriage.

I followed him and sat down. It was only after the train moved off that I noticed a lot of French troops and I wondered if we were on the right train. After travelling for a few hours we stopped and all the troops got out. We followed but there was no station

– nothing but open ground and we heard gunfire which was not far away.

I knew that we had taken the wrong train, and had gone off our course. We had landed near the French front. (Germany was still fighting after Austria gave in.)

We asked French officers when we could get a train for Paris, but most of them could not "savvy", till a French officer who could speak English told us we would get one in an hour's time.

The man I was with was a 2nd engineman and came from Great Yarmouth. We got to Paris all right and boarded another train for Boulogne, but when we tried to go aboard the boat to cross the Channel the officer at the gangway would not allow us without a pass. We explained to him that we were released naval prisoners from Austria, and he told us to go round the pier to the British Naval Authorities office and they would put us right.

When we arrived there we were asked if we wanted to go straight home but I said that I would rather go to my depot first at Devonport. I wanted a bath and some decent clothes as I was in a poor state. The officer there gave me five pounds and a pass to take me to Devonport. He also gave me my ration cards. I asked him what they were for and he said I would need them when I crossed the Channel as Britain was now on rations.

I had a bath and a good feed at Devonport and was issued with a new uniform. I felt like a new person.

I was there for two days and then sent on to Granton Naval Base in Scotland along with other naval men. We arrived at Granton about 1 am and slept on the waiting-room seats till 3 am. Then we took turns to go in and see the drafting officer.

When my turn came he ordered me to go aboard a certain trawler (mentioning the name) and I said, "No, sir."

He said "What?! Refusing duty?"

I said, "I am refusing duty because I am unfit for it after being a prisoner of war for over one and a half years."

So I was dismissed. I was then given leave home for over two months and shortly after that I was demobilised.

During my stay in Austria as a POW I found all officers and men very human and friendly, and some of the officers told me they did not like fighting against Britain. I know I was starving there and was punished for escaping but they were also starving. If I had been in other enemy countries my punishment would have been much more severe.

Recollections

I can still see myself, as a child aged seven or eight, standing by my great Auntie Lizzie's high box bed. I was reciting by rote "fisher folk family names" and going back eight generations. All the way back to Elizabeth Watson, who had "dried her tears and wrought". We were on our long summer holiday in my ancestors' house in Shore Street, Cellardyke.

Cellardyke held all I needed. We went nowhere else. Barefoot summers on hot pavements, my cousins "on tap", Jimmy Smith's shop, playing down the beach, over the back o' the pier, the cobbled wynd, cutsies, solid harbour walls, my Nana, the great aunts chattering, laughter, echoes of stories, all singing around the organ, bagatelle and the wind-up gramophone in the garret. It was the place we called Home.

In the 1950s, for me, "the May" was a distant dream: going out in a boat was not spoken of; "Don't go near the edge of the pier," they said – and that it wasn't a place to go alone. We swam "at the pond" no matter what the weather. Three times a day. It was bliss. I don't remember anyone mentioning the war memorial, ever, except for the view. I didn't wonder why there were a lot of women and fewer men.

As a young adult I walked in Kilrenny kirkyard, was shown my grandfather's grave. Later, I found John Bett's and others. We went to Chalmers Church but Nana never came; always busy with the dinner...

Later on, I wanted to find out more. (AEH, 2017)

Johnnie's World: Research Notes

John M. Smith's story stands as it was written. Reading his unembellished story led to research, the information being found in many places: from our family history – notes, handwritten stories and photographs; from relatives, friends, museum researchers, local books and the newspapers of the day; the internet – with articles, books and encyclopaedias online and WW1 forums.

The picture became clearer, with some dates added, but because of the very nature of war, and the passing of time, there is much still to be discovered. It's humbling to realise the effects on the people involved. Their influence is our legacy and is reflected in how we live our own lives today.

In Fife: By 1913, Cellardyke folk owned most of the 60 local steam drifters. With the ever-variable catches of the winter herring fishing, the summer fishing and the Yarmouth fishing – life was always challenging and busy in this close, tight-knit community.

August 1914 – Although the war was not generally expected, when it was announced, fishermen and others of all trades volunteered for active service.[1]

The previous winter herring fishing had been one of the best for years, but with the outbreak of war the fishing industry was badly affected. Boats were confined to harbour during darkness and there was a problem of insurance for those still involved in fishing.

For most people, daily life changed with the start of the war.

Many men had time on their hands, no wages, and needed to find other work. J. Corstorphine writes:

Most of the volunteers from the East Neuk of Fife joined the navy, where their seamanship proved to be of vital importance in the war effort. A large number of steam drifters were soon to be requisitioned by the Admiralty.

Some men volunteered but were not considered fit enough for active service so, as not all of the local fishing fleet went to war, they remained as fishermen during the hostilities, thus providing vital supplies of food.[2] Men of other trades mainly joined the local regiment, the Royal Highlanders, Black Watch.

On 3rd December 1914, the local newspaper *Coast Burgh's Observer* gave lists of Cellardyke, Anstruther and Pittenweem men who had already enlisted. My own grandfather, Thomas Watson – of 16 East Forth Street – is named there.

A few weeks later, on 14th January 1915, another local newspaper, the *East of Fife Record*, reported:

Cellardyke: Recruits for patrol vessels. On Thursday afternoon a public meeting was hurriedly called to hear Captain Hayward, Aberdeen, who had come down with the object of obtaining men to serve on patrol vessels working around the coast. Provost Black presided and briefly introduced Captain Hayward, who explained that he wanted men for patrol work on board drifters. The remuneration of deck hands amounted to about £2 per week and, after paying for their keep, the men had 33s or 34s [shillings] clear to themselves. Married men would receive separation allowance for their wives and families. About ten young men intimated their willingness to serve.

It is likely that my grandmother's brother, Cellardyke fisherman John Bett, attended the above meeting. He joined the Royal Naval Reserve (R.N.R.) as a deckhand on the steel steam drifter *Coreopsis*, KY116.

The fishermen, from an early age, were used to long days, sometimes with weeks and months at sea. A little insight is given by J. D. Leslie:[3]

> *At the age of nine Peter spent his first night at sea in the "Ruby" [owned by a Watson[4]] fishing boat – during the winter herring season off Anstruther. At twelve he was actually "gaun to sea" as boy cook in his uncle's boat during the summer "drave". From then[5] on until the early 20's he followed the vocation of fisherman, at home, in Shetland and North-eastern waters, at East Anglia, and off the west coast.*

It was a hard and dangerous way of life, the men and boys all dependent on each other and their combined knowledge, wisdom and intuition, for their livelihood – and, indeed, for their lives.

The *Coreopsis* (P. Gardner) left Anstruther in late January 1915, as did the *Dreel Castle* (W. Sutherland), *Golden Strand* (J. Stevenson), *Kilmany* (A. Gardner), *Guerdon* (Adam Reid), *Cromorna* (A. Henderson) and, of course, the *Craignoon* (A. Rodger). All had been enlisted for patrol duty.[6]

The Craignoon

The steam drifter *Craignoon*, KY279, was owned by members of the Rodger family. They were great nephews of Captain Alex Rodger of China Clipper fame, who was also great, great, great uncle to my grandmother, Alice Bett. The *Craignoon* was built in 1908, at Port Gordon, Moray, in the Geddes boat-building yard.

The name Craignoon also refers to a Cellardyke coastal area behind John Street, at one time a proposed new deep-water harbour.[7]

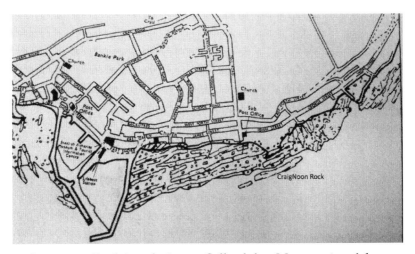

Craignoon Rock in relation to Cellardyke. Map reprinted from Stevenson, p. viii, with kind permission of Birlinn Press. Modified by Dave Smith to show exact location of the rock.

The women left behind during WW1, many being the wives or daughters of fishermen, were used to challenges, and the society was already somewhat matriarchal. They were emotionally strong and capable women who organised the family when the men were away at sea and had everything ready for when they returned. The nets had to be mended, but cleanliness and kindness were also high priorities. Women sometimes shared child-rearing duties, and those who had the gift to heal went to any home where healing was needed, with no fear.[8] Families were often large, and bereavement was no stranger, as can be seen in the local churchyards. Girls were expected to leave school if needed to "help at home". Older sisters were sometimes left to cope with the responsibilities of the whole household.[9]

Later on in WW1, older local girls were asked to leave their household responsibilities to work in ammunition factories for the war effort. It was a difficult time for all concerned, in the same way as it was for the men who had to leave their communities. However, it provided an opportunity, for both sexes, to travel further away from home and to mix with others from all over Britain.

As Kevin Dunion states – and as fishing communities world-wide know – the sea was able to take life, even without the help of the war. Many tales of loss, survival, suffering and gallantry can be found in the old books. George Gourlay gives long and detailed accounts of lives lost at sea, including that of my ancestor Henry Beat in 1865.[10]Another adventure well worth reading is that of the boat *Brothers*[11]in November 1875. It was said to be an unprecedented 40-day journey from Yarmouth to Anstruther, surviving fearful storms by a mixture of good seamanship, fortune and timely assistance.

Folk were well used to looking after those who had suffered the loss of "brave and useful lives". George Gourlay, in his late-nineteenth-century language, describes how help was at hand "during the anxious and weary days" and how it often came from those more well-off. He speaks of great kindness being shown "to soothe and comfort the lonely home, darkened by sorrow and despair".[12]The people of Kilrenny, Cellardyke and Anstruther were proud of their heritage and were determined and imaginative folk, who – especially when challenged – used their resources to the best. They "held their heads high" and lived up to the Royal Charter, given to the burgh in 1587 by King James.[13]

Around the Coast of Britain: On 7th August 1914 H.M.S. *Amphion* was sunk by a mine off Yarmouth.[14]On 20th October 1914 the first British merchant vessel, S.S. *Glitra,* was sunk in the North Sea by a German submarine and by 2nd November the

British government had declared the North Sea as a war zone. On 3rd November 1914 the British people experienced the first German naval raid on the British coast. This was near Gorleston and Yarmouth, striking at the very place that many East Neuk fishermen knew well.[15]

Fishing boats at Gorleston, near Great Yarmouth, back when fishermen would sail down from Cellardyke to benefit from the autumn herring fishing.

The Wider World: Military operations of the World War One took place in "seven theatres of war"[16] around the world, those being Western Europe (France and Flanders / Italy), The Balkans (Greek Macedonia, Serbia, Bulgaria and European Turkey /

Gallipoli [Dardanelles]), Russia, Egypt, Africa, Asia and Aus-tralasia. Concentrating even just on those places mentioned in Johnnie's story, it is interesting, and always humbling to read of countless heroic deeds and sacrifices. K Dunion sums up the magnitude of the operations thus: "The scale of conflict was such that in every community ordinary men… had done something extraordinary."[17]Those men had unimaginable experiences, and knowledge, that they often did not speak about afterwards.

Johnnie's Story begins in Anstruther: In January 1915, the skeleton crew – those first working on board the requisitioned *Craignoon* – are named as James Wilson, skipper, of Cellardyke; David Dunn, mate, of Pittenweem; Tom Duff, 1st engineer, from Alloa; John Smith, the 2nd engineer, from Anstruther; William McKenzie, deckhand, of Pittenweem, and John Corstorphine, deckhand, from Cellardyke. A steam drifter, when involved in fishing, would have had eight to ten men including an engineer and a fireman.[18]Skipper James Wilson, David Dunn, Tom Duff and our great uncle Johnnie (John Moncrieff Smith) remained on the Craignoon, but it seems that John Corstorphine left the drifter at Aberdeen before going to war in the Dardanelles.[19]

On board ship, men may have nicknames or be called by their surname, often to avoid confusion where two have the same name. War records are scanty and sometimes just not available, but newspaper articles from the time can sometimes give clarity.[20]Regarding William McKenzie, it was actually his brother Alex who, after joining the *Craignoon* at Falmouth, was to transfer ship to the *Morning Star*. Sadly, Alex's brother William had already died, on 22nd October in France.[21]

Off Cornwall: The base at Falmouth was named H.M.S. *Dreel Castle*, says Johnnie, after the steam drifter *Dreel Castle*, which was requisitioned in January 1915, as were many other local steam drifters, and used as a net minesweeper. The steam drifter *Dreel Castle* was also the parent ship of the patrols out of Falmouth. They were involved in patrolling, from late January – "a fine time" says Johnnie – along the Cornish coast. On holiday many years later, his wife Helen recorded in her diary how "he patrolled many a time round by Looe and Mevagissey" in the *Craignoon* during WW1.

To Gibraltar, then The Adriatic Sea: The *Craignoon*, and many other boats patrolling British waters, were to be sent further afield, and Johnnie writes about preparations being made to go to Gibraltar, presumably to the large British naval base constructed there in the late 1800s. Within days of the start of WW1, countries had been aligning themselves. On 6th August 1914 Austria-Hungary declared war on Russia, and Serbia declared war on Germany. Italy remained neutral then declared war on Austria-Hungary in May 1915, and this was where the *Craignoon* was destined to go: to join the Adriatic Campaign. Brindisi, on the Italian coast of the Adriatic Sea, was to be their base for a year or so, writes Johnnie. On 1st April 1915, *Craignoon* crew member Alex McKenzie was promoted from a deckhand to 2nd engineer and transferred to the steam drifter *Morning Star*, of Fraserburgh.[22] The *Wikipedia* entry for the Adriatic Campaign offers a neat summary of events:

> *In trying to protect Italy's eastern coast, the Allied forces mainly limited themselves to blockades, to try to stem the Austro-Hungarian bombardments and the forays of German and Austro-Hungarian submarines. This strategy was successful in regard to surface boats but failed in terms of U-boats, which had little trouble in this area for the whole of the war. Just before the start of WW1, an Anglo-French*

naval agreement was signed, allowing France to lead any
naval operations in the Mediterranean. Early on in the
war the Anglo-French force sunk S.M.S. Zenta, an Austro-
Hungarian cruiser, in the Battle of Antivari. During the
following weeks, small battles ensued, and both sides laid
extensive minefields. The fighting built up, ending in a long
but decisive defeat at Cattaro for the Allies in the autumn of
1914.

On 4th May 1915 it was agreed that an Allied fleet was to be created under the supreme command of the Italian navy, with the main base at Brindisi, which was also the main base for the Italian naval forces. A reserve fleet, partly based in Taranto, was to come under French supreme command.[23] Johnnie recounts how part of their time was spent patrolling off the coast of Albania, near the city of Durazzo, now renamed Durrës, and then back to Brindisi. Durrës and Brindisi are on opposite sides of one of the narrower points of the Adriatic Sea. In late December 1915 there was a naval battle fought off the coast of Durazzo, the First Battle of Durazzo, which resulted in an Allied victory.[24]

On 7th / 8th January 1916, in the Adriatic Sea, an Italian transport ship, *Citta di Palermo*, struck a mine as she was leaving Brindisi for Durazzo. There were 200 on board, the majority being British. It was said that it was only because of swift action by the crews of a group of steam drifters that about half of the lives were saved. Unfortunately, during the rescue of survivors, three of the drifters themselves struck mines, resulting in the loss of their crews. The unlucky drifters were *Frenchy*, *Cravenwood* and *Morning Star*.[25] The *Craignoon* was not involved, being elsewhere, but Johnnie writes that all were saddened to hear the news as one of their crew, Alex McKenzie, had transferred to the *Morning*

Star. Besides Alex McKenzie, the casualties of the *Morning Star* included Skipper Peter Buchan and his son, also called Peter, aged 16. Alex, aged 35, the first Pittenweem naval victim of the war, "was quiet, frank and of an obliging disposition."[26] He left a widow and four young children. Anstruther steam drifter *Evening Star* (KY 189, owned by R Hughes) took part in the same rescue on 8th January 1916.[27] The Cellardyke-born skipper John Hughes was also decorated for his earlier involvement in sinking an Austrian submarine. The 17th August *East of Fife Record* reads:

> *The skipper and mate of the Evening Star are sons of Mr Robert Hughes, fisherman, of John Street, and he and the family are naturally proud of the gallantry displayed by their sons in the rescue of life. It is now 14 months since they went out on patrol service, and the family consider that it is about time they were getting home on leave for a brief period.*

It seems that "leave", if given to the ordinary sailors and soldiers, happened only infrequently.[28] It is possible to imagine that the logistics in bringing a crew member home from, say, the Balkans – whilst their steam drifters were still involved in operations – was difficult, and probably not a priority.

Johnnie writes about the *Craignoon* being transferred to the base at Taranto, in the Gulf of Taranto, Southern Italy, with duties in the Strait of Otranto. The strait connects the Adriatic Sea with the Ionian Sea and separates Italy from Albania. The barrage was an attempt to blockade the Adriatic Sea to obstruct Austro-Hungarian ships from going to the Mediterranean. Austrian destroyers frequently made raids on the line of drifters, often in darkness.

The idea of this barrage originated from Winston Churchill in

May 1915, when Italy joined the war against Austria-Hungary. On his website, Russell Phillips writes how the concept was implemented:

> *Churchill offered to supply 50 fishing trawlers and 50 miles of submarine indicator nets, in return for the Italians providing crews and armament. The Italians declined, realising that manning and arming the craft would be a significant challenge. [The Adriatic is 45 miles wide (72km) at the Strait of Otranto.]... The drifters were organised into three divisions of 20. At any one time, two divisions would be deployed with their nets, while the third would be in Brindisi. Two drifters from each division would be at a subsidiary base at Taranto for docking, boiler cleaning, and repairs. The Italians provided a pair of merchant ships (Gallipoli & Adratico) and a small auxiliary steamer (Mazzini) armed with three six-pounders and used for inspections, mail delivery, etc.*

On one occasion, as the *Craignoon* was in the Otranto Barrage, with steam drifters in a line between Brindisi and Corfu, there was an attack of heavy gunfire close by. It was 1st June 1916. The *Craignoon* left its position in the barrage and steamed towards the firing, only to find that the Fraserburgh drifter *Beneficient*, one of their group, was just a pile of wreckage with no survivors.[29] George McKay was the skipper of another drifter in the same group, the *Helenora*, (S group)[30] and he later wrote how it was, in that moment, proved to him that a drifter could "go up" rather than "go down", and why there were no survivors of the Beneficient. It must have been tough to know that, with only a small gun, which was hardly any way of defending themselves against the destroyers, the crews of the drifters were almost sitting targets.

Skipper James Wilson at Anstruther Harbour.

They were courageous men, and, after the war, all were awarded their war medals. For his brave actions in the Adriatic during WW1, Cellardyke-born Skipper James Brunton Wilson was also awarded a gold medal "for meritorious conduct" and "for an action that took place on 23rd July 1916". The certificate states: "Grand Order of Peter 1st, Awarded by King Alexander of Serbia" and is signed 6th May 1921.[31] King Peter was the supreme commander of the Serbian army in WW1, and his second son Alexander was his heir.

By August 1st, 1916, two years into the war, Russia had fared poorly, losing control of territory, while Serbia had been overrun. A small Allied force had seized Salonika in Greece to try to maintain a token force in the Balkans. At this time, the Otranto Barrage was in place, running between Brindisi and Corfu, across the Strait of Otranto.

When Serbia was overrun by the Austro-Hungarian army in the winter of 1915, Peter 1st and his army had retreated across Albania. Due to poor weather and lack of food, not just for the army but also for the retreating civilians, the circumstances of the retreat were dreadful:

> *All told, only some 155,000 Serbs, mostly soldiers, reached the coast of the Adriatic Sea and embarked on Allied transport ships that carried the army to various Greek islands (many to Corfu) before being sent to Salonika.*[32]

The first Serbian troops landed at Corfu mid-January 1916, in very poor condition, and the retreat was complete by mid-February 1916, when the Serbians set up their government at Corfu. The depleted Serbian army travelled by sea to Salonika (Thessaloniki) in April 1916, after the Greek government had refused them an overland route.

Some might say that Serbia was actually to blame for the start of WW1; in 2014 Dr. Heather Jones, LSE, gave her opinion:

A handful of bellicose political and military decision-makers in Austria-Hungary, Germany and Russia caused WW1. Relatively common before 1914, assassinations of royal figures did not normally result in war. But Austria-Hungary's military hawks – principal culprits for the conflict – saw the Sarajevo assassination of the Austro-Hungarian Archduke Franz Ferdinand and his wife by a Bosnian Serb as an excuse to conquer and destroy Serbia, an unstable neighbour which sought to expand beyond its borders into Austro-Hungarian territories. Serbia, exhausted by the two Balkan wars of 1912–13 in which it had played a major role, did not want war in 1914.[33]

The Balkans was an unstable area in 1914. The leaders of Europe "failed to avoid a disaster. One that would engulf the world and shatter world order".[34]Johnnie and his contemporaries were paying the price for this failure, showing courage and self-discipline in most trying circumstances.

The job of manning the Otranto Barrage was dangerous but monotonous, as referred to in notes concerning Skipper Joseph Watts, of drifter *Gowanlea*:

Transferred to Italy in 1915, Watt served on drifters enduring boring patrol work keeping Austrian submarines from breaking into the Mediterranean Sea. During this time he was highly commended, for his role in the operation to evacuate the remnants of the Serbian army following their defeat and retreat to Albania in January 1916 for which he was later awarded the Serbian Gold Medal.[35]

Perhaps all Otranto Barrage skippers received this award. There were many tales of bravery rewarded, and most of the facts and figures came from the local newspapers. By 1918 Skipper David Watson had collected the Italian Medal of Military Valour, The French Croix de Guerre and the Serbian Gold Medal.[36]

The following account tells of one brave "adventure" for the crew of the *Craignoon*. Whilst returning from the Otranto Barrage to base with the group, the drifter altered course and headed towards a floating mine on orders from the skipper, James Wilson, who had spotted the mine. Johnnie writes that it was "usual for them to fire a six-pound shell from their 50mm Italian gun, which would then make a hole in the mine and cause it to sink to the bottom". This time they went a little too close to the mine and the shot struck one of the plungers – so that the mine blew up, with a piece of it ending up on board! With the noise of the explosion and the smoke, the rest of S group initially thought that the *Craignoon* had been lost, but their luck was to hold until May of the next year.

Early on 15th May 1917 the line of drifters, 47 of them at that time, were attacked by the Austro-Hungarian navy.

On the night of 14th May 1917, the Austro-Hungarian navy launched their largest raid on the barrage. The raid was carried out by the cruisers Novara, Helgoland, and Saida supported by the destroyers Csepel, Balaton and U-boats U4 and U27, along with German U-boat UC-25, under the command of Admiral Miklós Horthy. A supporting force composed of the armoured cruiser Sankt Georg, two destroyers, and several torpedo boats was on standby. The old pre-dreadnought battleship Budapest and a screen of torpedo boats were also available. As the force sailed south, they encountered and attacked a small Italian convoy, sinking a destroyer and a munitions ship, and setting another ship on fire, causing it to be abandoned. The Austro-Hungarian force began the attack on the barrage at 03:30, usually warning the drifter crews to abandon ship before opening fire. Forty-seven drifters were on the barrage when the force attacked, of which fourteen were sunk and four were damaged. The remaining drifters withdrew until the Austro-Hungarians returned to port.[37]

Johnnie writes of the *Craignoon* having no escape, with two enemy cruisers on the west side and one enemy cruiser on the east side. They had already witnessed one drifter gun crew being shot – and their small gun was no match against these armed cruisers. The crew put out their small boat and got into it, with Skipper James Wilson coming aboard last. After pulling away from the *Craignoon* as fast as they could they then watched – as their ship blew up into tiny pieces.

George McKay, skipper of the *Helenora*, watched the *Craignoon* and two other drifters sink. He writes that they were rowing towards the land (Johnnie's account informs us that they were to the west of Faro Island) in their small boat and the crews of the *Avondale*, *Craignoon* and *Serene* were in three other small boats. He gives a detailed description of how the boats went down:

The first one was the "Avondale." She had been hit somewhere about the engine-room, and she went down quickly stern first, the fore end of her rising all the time out of the water until I could see seven or eight feet of her keel. The next to

49

do down was the "Craignoon" or I ought rather to say "to go up." She got two shells into her boiler in quick succession and in less time that it takes me to say she went up in the air in a thousand pieces, the debris was falling from her, all around us. Since I went on duty in the Adriatic I had seen many good ships blown up by mines, and to have seen the "Craignoon" go up in the air, the way she did, anyone would have actually thought she had struck a mine. This also proves to me how most of the drifter "Beneficient's" crew were killed when she was shelled by one of the three enemy destroyers about twelve months before this time. The "Serene" was the last of the three to sink. She had been hit somewhere about the wheelhouse and she gradually settled down by the head, her stern meanwhile rising, so that I saw nearly half her keel.

After the Austro-Hungarian navy cruiser *Novara* had sunk the *Craignoon*, the four drifter crews in their small boats watched her sinking other drifters. Then the *Novara* came after the men in their small boats, but not to kill them. The crews were lucky to escape with their lives that day, and it's difficult to see how they could have chosen to do anything differently. The Austro-Hungarian navy certainly meant business, and the likelihood of injury or death was a grim fact. Just the night before, an enemy U-boat "had laid a minefield at the mouth of Brindisi Harbour; the French destroyer Boutefeu struck one of these mines exiting the harbour the very same day and exploded, sinking with all hands."[38]

Amongst the many medals awarded for bravery during this action, on 15th May 1917, Skipper Joseph Watt of Fraserburgh, of the drifter *Gowanlea*, received the Victoria Cross. Russell Phillips writes of his bravery:

Some drifters chose to fight, most notably the Gowan Lee [sic]. When ordered by Helgoland to surrender and abandon ship, the captain, Joseph Watt, ordered full speed ahead and called on the crew to give three cheers and fight to the finish. The crew managed to get a single shot off before their six-pounder was disabled, but they kept working to get the gun firing again, despite being under heavy fire. The Gowan Lea [sic] was heavily damaged but remained afloat. She picked up survivors from other drifters that had been sunk and came alongside Floandi to remove her dead and wounded. Joseph Watt was awarded the Victoria Cross for his "most conspicuous gallantry". One of the crew received the Conspicuous Gallantry Medal and two received the Distinguished Service Medal for their parts in the action.[39]

In the early morning light, the Austro-Hungarian cruiser *Novara* picked up the crews from the steam drifters *Craignoon*, *Avondale*, *Serene* and *Helenora*, on ropes hanging over the side of the ship. Once on board the crews were treated well, but their ordeal under fire was about to begin again! As the *Novara* made its way towards the Austro-Hungarian base at Cattaro (now known as Kotor), the British gave chase. At about 9 am the crew, now prisoners on an enemy ship, were told that the cruisers *Liverpool*, *Dartmouth* and *Bristol* were close by. When the firing began, with shells exploding all around and within the ship, Johnnie writes of hearing the cries of the dying and wounded men. His story is detailed and needs no more explanation, save to say that the experience must have been terrifying.

Dartmouth—faster than Bristol—closed to effective engagement range with the Austro-Hungarian ships, and opened fire. A shell from Dartmouth struck Novara, at which point the Austro-Hungarian ships laid a smoke screen in order to close the distance. Dartmouth was struck several times, and by 11:00, Acton[40] ordered the ship to reduce speed to allow Bristol to catch up. Novara was hit several more times, and her main feed pumps and starboard auxiliary steam pipe had been damaged, which caused the ship to begin losing speed. At 11:05, Acton turned away in an attempt to separate Saida from Novara and Helgoland. At this point, Sankt Georg was approaching the scene, which prompted Acton to temporarily withdraw to consolidate his forces. This break in the action was enough time for the Austro-Hungarians to save the crippled Novara; Saida took the ship under tow while Helgoland covered them. Unaware that Novara had been disabled, and fearing that his ships would be drawn too close to the Austrian naval base at Cattaro, Acton broke off the pursuit. The destroyer Acerbi misread the signal, and attempted to launch a torpedo attack, but was driven off by the combined fire of Novara, Saida, and Helgoland. At 12:05, Acton realised the dire situation Novara was in, but by this time, the Sankt Georg group was too close. The Sankt Georg group rendezvoused with Novara, Saida, and Helgoland, and Csepel and Balaton reached the scene as well. The entire group returned to Cattaro together.[41]

Johnnie writes that the casualties on board the *Novara* were 15 killed and 25 wounded. He says that it was about 7 pm when the *Novara* arrived in Cattaro and almost dark when "they were taken up on deck to be taken ashore", but their long day, of 15th May, was not yet over. His story tells of a long walk[42] to an old Montenegrin fortress, probably one of the remains of the earlier fortification in the region, and of sleeping on straw in an open shed. After meeting up with other drifter crews there were 72 men altogether. Two enginemen from the Buckie drifter *Quarry Knowe* had died.

At this time, and for a good while longer, food was short and the men were on "starvation" rations, in the same way as the Austrians themselves were starving. The "officers" (skippers and first mates) were treated in the same way, initially. Skipper George McKay of the sunken drifter *Helenora* wrote:

> *Next morning, the 16th, at 6.0 a.m. we were roused by the sentries for breakfast, which consisted of black coffee, no sugar or milk and no bread. After we had our coffee they gave us the privilege of a wash but forgetting to give us any soap or a towel. We were then marched into a backyard for exercise which consisted of lying or standing about until 11.0 a.m. when we were given a portion of bread, half maize, weighing about ¾ lb. to each man. Half an hour later we were lined up for dinner, which consisted of some sort of soup made with sour cabbage and something like dried grass. We were told that we were getting the same rations as their own soldiers and we found this to be true. For as bad as the food was, I have seen, more than once, soldiers going to the drain and gathering up and eating what our fellows had thrown away. The country was in a terrible state of starvation.*

McKay goes on to say that he "asked one of the officers if we could get a letter written to our people to inform them that we were well and where we were but was told that we could not write home until we arrived at our camp. We would be leaving for our camp in a couple of days, but in the meantime he would take our addresses and try to get word to England through the Red Cross in France." Even before the Admiralty itself had official notification of the men's whereabouts, their grieving families were reassured as to their safety.[43]

News arrives – from Austria to Anstruther: On 26th May 1917, a report from the Admiralty was published in local newspaper *The Fishing News*. Details of the action are given and also details of the drifters sunk: where registered and registration number, tonnage, date of build and owners. The official list of casualties includes the news that the Austrian report showed 72 prisoners. In *The Fishing News*, 26th May 1917, six men were reported as having been killed, and are named as:

Bell, William John, deckhand R.N.R. 7520 D.A.
Boulton, James, deckhand R.N.R. 13230 D.A.
Cowrie, John, deckhand, R.N.R. 6102 D.A.
Fowler, William Herne, engineman, R.N.R. 2439 E.S.
Gordon, Adam, second hand, R.N.R. 3945 D.A.
Harris, Douglas Morris, able seaman, R.N.V.R., Bristol Z9359.

In the same report, ten men were reported as wounded and 68 were reported missing. Besides Skipper James Wilson, of the original six crew of the *Craignoon* there are three names on the list of those missing:

Duff, Thomas, engineman, R.N.R. 2032 E.S.
Dunn, David, second hand, R.N.R. 1165 S.A.
Smith, John, engineman, R.N.R. 2033 R.S.

Prisoners of War: Meanwhile, in Austria, the men from the steam drifters were by this time at the town of Graz, being housed temporarily in an old prison. Graz, which had been Archduke Ferdinand's home town, is to the south east of Austria and is now the second-largest city in Austria.[44]

The journey to Graz, via Sarajevo, was cold and uncomfortable, with very little food and, according to Johnnie, took "three days and three nights" in cattle trucks. However, the skippers and the four 1st enginemen travelled in proper carriages. The Austrians had made a mistake with the ratings, as George McKay explains:

The cruiser that captured the crews of the "Avondale," "Craig-noon," "Serene" and "Helenora" was the "Novara." When we got on board we explained to the officer who questioned us, what our ratings were. The skippers were Warrant Officers. The Mate, 1st engineman and 2nd engineman were rated as Petty Officers with the Mate the next in turn to take charge. When we went to Castlenova the officer told us that the four skippers and the four 1st enginemen would be sent to a different camp to the crew, meaning an officer's camp. He said, as for the other two officers from each ship they would have to go along with the crews. We four skippers with our 1st enginemen travelled in second class carriages, whilst the rest of the men all travelled in cattle trucks, twenty-five to thirty men in a truck.

In WW1 Austria-Hungary, rank, and nationality made quite a difference to how prisoners of war (POWs) were treated. Before the train journey, the "officers" from the steam drifters were given money and made to understand that they would be able to buy food at any of the station restaurants along the railway line, and mostly had meals in good restaurants.[45] The rest of the men suffered from starvation and were only given a bowl of sauerkraut and a piece of bread once each day. One day the train stopped at a soldier's camp and each man received a bowl of potato soup, instead of the usual sauerkraut, which, according to Johnnie, relieved the monotony.

Apparently, only been since 1990 has there been focused and rigorous research into the treatment of POWs in Austria-Hungary. Facts and figures were not given in full after the end of the war, and the extent of the huge numbers of deaths from starvation and epidemics in the camps was not fully appreciated. The treatment was mostly humanitarian, but initially the huge numbers of POWs arriving in the camps caused an impossible situation. The camps became less crowded when forced labour was introduced in 1915, as a large proportion of each camp's POWs was sent away for work projects elsewhere.[46]

The Russian and Italian POWs were in a very vulnerable situation as they did not receive support from their home countries. British POWs were more fortunate. Many wrote letters home to tell family and friends that they were starving. Although their loved ones sent supplies, apparently many packages did not reach their destination or were poorly packed. Others had secret messages hidden in the food, so they were destroyed by the enemy.

During the war the British Red Cross and the Order of St John worked together. Through the Central Prisoners of War Committee they co-ordinated relief for British POWs. Every prisoner would receive an adequate supply of food and clothing. Parcels of food, each weighing about 10 pounds, were delivered fortnightly to every prisoner who had been registered. By the end of World War One, over 2.5 million parcels had been organised, packaged, wrapped and despatched to prisoners of war in camps abroad.[47]

Johnnie, and the other POWs from the steam drifters, had to endure about three months of suffering with the Austrian "starvation diet" before the food parcels started to arrive.

Johnnie writes about 25 days spent in the quarantine prison at Graz; with hindsight, perhaps the quarantine measures had been put in place to counter the camp epidemics. He tells of how they were starved and then "marched around the town as a show piece, to give the impression that Britain was starving and in a bad way". He says that they were "a pitiful sight", hardly able to manage the walk which lasted for about an hour. However, something suddenly happened which showed the "mettle" of the men, their determination or spirit – and it was singing, "good singing from seventy voices". This put "new life" into the men.

The relatives at home probably already knew that their men were being brave and cheerful. An earlier newspaper account, on 24th September 1915, reported:

> *Our boys are a cheery lot, and great on music... the voices of Anstruther and Cellardyke boys can be depended upon to strike up a tune, which is lustily taken up by the whole company. It is a cheery sound, and keeps our spirits up wonderfully.*

This account was provided for the *East of Fife Record* by Captain C.H. Maxwell of the 1/7th Black Watch. It must have been somewhat heartening for those "waiting on news" back at home to be able to read such comments. My own grandfather, Thomas Watson, was one of those serving in the Black Watch at this time.[48]He was a member of the Anstruther Philharmonic Choir.

Although, by mid-May 1917, the war at sea was over for Johnnie, his WW1 story is only really beginning at this stage! There was a long struggle with starvation, travelling to, and escaping from, POW camps.

On 21st June 1917, they arrived at their first "proper" POW camp, which was in Deutsch Gabel,[49]Bohemia (until 1918 part of the Austro-Hungarian monarchy). This camp was for merchant seamen and under Austrian administration. The town is now called Jablonné v Podještědí (German: *Gabel*). It is in Liberec District, Liberec Region, Czech Republic.[50]Johnnie described it as a good camp, where eventually their health returned. It was in this camp, by about mid-September 1917, that letters started to arrive from home. Money from relatives could be included in these letters. Red Cross parcels of food and tobacco arrived at about the same time and, gradually, the men's health began to improve.

The Austrians noticed the improvement in the men's health and it was decided to make them work. The next camp, Laibach,[51]was for enforced labour, and all except the skippers and first engine-men were sent there, joining many Russians and Italians. The Russians did not get the food parcels which continued for the British, and Johnnie tells of how "it was a common thing for some of them to drop dead of starvation". The Laibach camp was almost certainly Schloss Laibach, Ljubljana, Austria (now Slovenia).

There was a great deal of misery in Laibach, and the work for most was hard. Johnnie describes the camp as being "unhealthy" and tells of "being sick of seeing so much suffering".

Johnnie Decides to Escape: His escape route, with one other man, was through forests and by train, was from Laibach towards Trieste and lasted for seven days. The story gives detail as to the extent of their journey, and, when they were recaptured, a German general was fooled by how far the pair had travelled. If, indeed, they had made it from Deutsch Gabel to Trieste, it would have been about 450 miles. As it was, their journey from Laibach towards Trieste, now an Italian port, was nearer 50 miles.

The pair were returned to Deutsch Gabel for punishment, and then Johnnie was re-assigned to the camp at Laibach, making him determined that he would attempt a second escape. His freedom on this occasion was shorter, from a railway station at Reichenburg,[52] part way between Deutsch Gabel and Laibach. Reichenburg, in this context, is likely to be Liberec, now a town in the Czech Republic.

Vienna: After more severe punishment for this second escape, Johnnie was sent to an officers' camp near Vienna. He waited to see if he needed to escape again, but found that it was "a good, clean, healthy camp" and his job there as an orderly for officers wasn't too arduous. However, he was "now on the Austrian starvation diet" again and did not expect to receive any more food parcels or tobacco. As his detailed story reveals, he had to use his ingenuity to survive.

On November 11th 1918,[53] Austria-Hungary's part in World War One ended with complete military collapse, even if at the time all forces were standing outside of borders of 1914 rather than having retreated. With the failure of the army came the disintegration of Austria-Hungary in general.

Freedom at Last: Johnnie tells of his return journey home. It was an eventful journey, especially when he took a wrong train and ended up hearing gunfire, somewhere near the French front. At last he was given better directions and went by train to Paris, then to Boulogne before crossing the channel. Once back on British soil, Johnnie chose to go to Plymouth, to his previous base at Devonport. He wanted to tidy himself up – and to have a good meal!

Johnnie was then sent to Granton Naval Base, in the Firth of Forth, Scotland. He wasn't with the other ex-POW sailors, and there may have been some mistake, because he was told to report for duty on a trawler. Although not fit to work, he almost got into trouble for refusing an order! At last, Home Leave was given – after which he was demobilised. At the end of his story as a World War One Sailor, Johnnie looks back and comments about the humanity and kindness shown by his guards during his time as a POW in Austria.

AEH, 2017

Appendix 1: The Royal Naval Reserve

There were three sections of the Royal Naval Reserve (R.N.R.), in 1914, with local seafaring men generally joining the first category. JeffH01, an *Ancestry* forum poster, describes them thus:

1. The Royal Naval Reserve (R.N.R.) – formed after the Royal Naval Reserve Act 1859, the R.N.R. provided a pool of trained seamen recruited from merchant seaman and fishermen via local shipping offices.

2. Royal Naval Reserve Trawler Section (R.N.R.[T]) – formed in 1911 when it was realised the R.N.R. was mainly men with deep sea experience and in wartime there would be a need to use trawlers as patrol boats and mine sweepers and the R.N.R.[T] was to provide the men and vessels for that. Only employing fishermen, the R.N.R.[T] was separate from the R.N.R. until 1921. Note when trawlers were requisitioned it was complete with crew, who were entered on a form T124.

3. Royal Naval Volunteer Reserve (R.N.V.R.) – formed in 1903, this was a force of volunteers who could be "called" during an emergency or war. Unlike the professional seamen of the R.N.R., in peacetime, VR volunteers took part in naval training on a "part-time" basis, holding down civilian jobs that were usually unrelated to vessels or the sea. The R.N.V.R. was main source of officers and men during the wars. Men of the R.N.V.R. also served as infantry in WW1 in the Royal Naval Division.[54]

Regarding the letters after each man's service number – when joining the R.N.R., men had to prove that they had previous experience in their work to be accepted. Some commonly held post-nominal letters for the R.N.R. are:

- DA = Deck Hands; SD = Deck Hands (Special Trawler Section); DE = Deck Hands (Trawler Reserve Emergency Section)
- ES = Enginemen; EX = Enginemen (Trawler Reserve Emergency Section)
- SA = Second Hands; SE = Second Hands (Trawler Reserve Emergency Section)
- SB = Boys; BE = Boys (Trawler Reserve Emergency Section); SBC = Boy Cooks
- TS = Trimmers; ST = Trimmers (Special Trawler Section); TE = Trimmers (Trawler Reserve Emergency Section);
- TC = Trimmer Cooks; CE = Trimmer Cooks (Trawler Reserve Emergency Section)
- WSE = Skippers (Trawler Reserve Emergency Section)[55]

Appendix 2: Uncle Johnnie and Wartime Contemporaries

John Moncrieff Smith, known as Johnnie, was born at Anstruther in 1896, the son of David Smith, marine engineer, and Cellardyke-born Elizabeth Moncrieff. The family had moved south from Aberdeenshire to Shore Street, Anstruther, via Stonehaven in 1891 or 1892. He was the sixth child in a family of five boys and three girls and was born number at 42 Shore Street, Anstruther, which was above what was to become Brattisani Ice Cream Parlour and the famous fish and chip shop Anstruther Fish Bar.

Johnnie and his mum, Elizabeth Smith (née Moncrieff).

At the outbreak of WW1, in 1914, Johnnie was 18 years old. After registering as a second engineer with the R.N.R., he started active service in January 1915.

Standing L–R: George Smith, Johnnie Smith, Georgina Cormack,
unknown, Mary Smith, Tommie Smith. Seated: unknown, unknown.

In the above photo, George is wearing the local regiment uniform of the Black Watch, as is Tommie. Johnnie is in naval uniform. Later, Georgina became Tommie's wife and they emigrated to America. Mary Smith married David Lowrie and both went to Africa as missionaries.[56]

The "wartime" wedding photograph of David Smith and Mary Watson, who married at the Palace Hotel, Edinburgh, in August 1918. Standing L–R: Tommie Smith, David Smith, Mary Watson. Sitting: Helen Watson, Georgina Cormack.

David was three years older than Johnnie and also a marine engineer. Mary was Nellie's older sister, and this meant that by the time Johnnie and Nellie married, two of the Smith brothers had married two of the Watson sisters!

Helen Watson, always known as Nellie, was born in Cellardyke in 1895, the daughter of a fisherman. Her mother and father were Catherine (Kate) Smith and William Watson, who married in 1888.[57]William was skipper of the *Midlothian* and later skipper/owner of the steam drifter *Violet* (KY 251).

Nellie was second child in a family of two girls and two boys. First the family lived at 20 Rodger Street, later moving to 16 East Forth Street, which was the Watson family home. Sadly, Kate died when the family was still young, and so Mary took responsibility and "kept house" for the family, from the age of 17.

At the outbreak of WW1 Nellie was almost 19 years old. She was probably working as a seamstress at the local oilskin and clothing factory.

Girls all over Britain were asked to support the war effort. Two best friends, Nellie and Alice, were recruited from Cellardyke as "housekeepers". They worked in a residential hostel, looking after the "munitionettes", the girls who were employed in munition (ammunition) factories.[58]

Personal family notes from Alice's daughter Joan Kingscott (also Johnnie's niece) give some insight into Nellie and Alice's time in the munitions factory:

> *Sometimes Mum had to rise at 4am to make porridge for the girls. Auntie Nellie says she used to go round with the bell to wake the girls up. They scrubbed stairs and floors, did general cleaning and waited at tables. Everyone had to wash up for one hundred girls and the plates were higher than Babs, the scullery maid. At night Babs danced and when they heard matron coming they jumped into bed with their clothes on!*[59]

Nellie is seated and Alice is standing.

The photograph of the two of them has more of Joan's words on the back: "Auntie Nellie, Alice Bett (mum) working as housemaids in the hostel where the munition girls lived. Auntie May went too. They made their own outfits."

It was necessary to wear more utilitarian clothes when working in a munitions factory. Despite the grim reality of the ammunition stacked in the background, Nellie (L) and Alice (R) are obviously feeling amused by having their photographs taken in these outfits!

Alice Pratt Bett (my grandmother), known as Ailass, was a quiet and lovely person with a sense of humour and a quick wit.

All her long life, children especially loved her and were "drawn to" her.

By the time Ailass was 15, the family were living at 11 Shore Street, Cellardyke.[60] Ailass's older sister Lizzie was a sewing machinist at the oilskin factory and older brother John was a deckhand (see below for more on John). Ailass was a frustrated academic, having been made to leave school when she desperately wanted to continue. Her mother 'needed her at home' and there was nothing Ailass could do about it. At Cellardyke Public School, a teacher wrote to Ailass's parents and even made a visit to the house, to no avail, telling the parents that if she stayed, Ailass would get the 'Dux'.[61]

So, Ailass had to stay home to help out. A big part of her work was to mend the torn fishing nets, which were hoisted up into the garret. Certificates show that she attended classes for those who had left school. She was musical, being in the Philharmonic Choir and teaching herself to play the family harmonium. Escaping from the garret occasionally to 'play the organ' was a relief, she told us, to combat the drudgery and monotony of mending the nets.

In early 1915, when Ailass was 19 years old, her father's boat *The Alices* was requisitioned by the government and the "net-mending" came to an abrupt end. When the appeal came to Cellardyke for girls to help the war effort, Ailass signed up. (See Helen Watson)

Thomas Smith Watson (my grandfather), known as Tom, was born at 20 Rodger Street, Cellardyke, in 1897, third child and first son. He was Mary and Nellie's brother, son of fisherman William Watson (the *Violet*) and Catherine (Kate) Smith. Tom did not follow his father into 'the fishing', choosing instead the trade of cabinetmaker.[62]

When WW1 started in August 1914, Tom was just 17 years old. He was amongst the first from Cellardyke to volunteer and joined the 1st Battalion of the Black Watch in September 1914.

We have my grandfather's kilt, over one hundred years old, and testimony to quality material.

The fabric was re-sewn and made into a picnic rug after the war and is mentioned in a poem, written by my mother, Joan Bett Watson, who was Tom's daughter and his only child.

Tom Watson, with the kilt that became a rug. This photograph was taken at the start of the First World War. Tom attended training camps before being sent to France.

'A Black Watch Soldier' (1914–1918)

By Joan Kingscott (née Watson)

My Dad joined up at seventeen,
To go to war he was so keen,
He chose the Black Watch Regiment
With a bed at night – a simple tent.
All hell let loose going 'over the top'
For Jerry kept them 'on the hop'.
The smell of death lay all around
While gunfire made a deafening sound.
Brave hearts stood firm against all fear
'T'will be all over in a year'
Young lives were spent to set us free
That price was paid for you and me
My Father's kilt became a rug
Something to treasure, something to hug.[63]

A Black Watch training camp. Tom Watson is on the ground at front right. This photograph shows some variety of uniform, including hats.

Tom Watson, on leave, with a fellow WW1 soldier.

During the war Tom became a signaller. He also qualified as an Assistant Instructor of Signalling in April 1916, by which time he was a Lieutenant/Corporal. The certificate states that during the six-week course at Dalkeith Scottish Command Signal School, Tom was examined in the theory and practice of Signalling, Telephony, Map-Reading and Despatch-Riding.

Tom's "Certificate of Employment" given at the end of November 1918, is good to read – especially as I didn't meet him: "During the time I have known this man, I have always found him to be a thoroughly reliable, hardworking and efficient soldier."[64]

Tom's private view, in the light of experience, was that the war had been "wasted years".

John Bett was born in Cellardyke in 1893, the second child of Henry Bett, a fisherman (skipper/owner), and Annie Barclay of Shore Street. Henry and Annie had four children but John was their only son.

After leaving Cellardyke School, he worked as a deckhand and fisherman on his father's boat, *The Alices* (KY210), an 84-ton wooden steam drifter.

The Alices leaving Anstruther Harbour.

Left: John Bett at Yarmouth. Right: John's Sisters: Lizzie, Annie &
Alice.

In August 1914, in a local newspaper report, John was described as "a Cellardyke youth" who had dived into Cellardyke Harbour to save a boy called Alex Ritchie, who had fallen in.[65] John's identity, in this instance, was confirmed by my distant cousin Harry Watson. He checked for John Bett in Cellardyke in the 1911 census and explained: "Out of 5 men and boys with that name the only one who could be described as a 'youth' was a John Bett who was 18 in 1911. Sure enough, he turned out to be John Bett of 11 Shore Street, brother of Alice, your granny."

John volunteered and joined the R.N.R. In January 1915 he left Anstruther on the *Coreopsis*. He was not to return to his native shores, and was one of the first "sons of Cellardyke" to be lost in the war.

The *Coreopsis* was on patrol off the coast of County Antrim on 20th April 1915 when tragedy struck. The family story – handed down by word of mouth when they could bear to speak of him – told that John was ordered, with other men, to use a small boat to retrieve an anchor in the midst of a storm. The crew knew that it was too dangerous, and that they should not be sent on such a mission, but there was no choice but to obey the order. It was said that the captain was inexperienced and mistaken. John was known to be a strong swimmer, which made his drowning more inexplicable.

A single postcard, neatly written in pencil, beginning with *Dear Mother and Father* and ending with *From your loving son John* was to be the final communication, kept in sadness. The effects of WW1 on the small communities would have been huge, as it was for each and every family who suffered a loss. John's mother, Annie Barclay, grieved and wore black for "a' her days".

The following account was given to Kevin Dunion by my late uncle, Sonny Corstorphine:

> *The sea rather than enemy attack was to blame when another 22 year old from Cellardyke was being mourned after five members of the crew of the patrol boat Coreopsis, stationed at Larne, were swept into the water off the Irish coast at Antrim. Accounts of what happened differ, as they so often do in war. Newspapers reported the heroic efforts made by the boat's engineer to save the men and 4 were rescued but despite diving repeatedly into the sea he was unable to save deckhand John Bett who drowned. After 4 hours of searching his body was recovered and he was brought home to be buried at Kilrenny Churchyard.[66] His family were left to wonder*

why he had been endangered in the first place having been told that he had been put into a small boat to recover an anchor and, in the middle of a gale, the boat had capsized.[67]

John Bett's memorabilia, including a large framed portrait, is now at the Scottish Fisheries Museum, Anstruther.

Thomas Smith, known as Tom, was the first-born son of fisherman William Smith (skipper of the *Olive Leaf*) and Margaret (Maggie) Bruce and the eldest in a family of four sons and one daughter. Tom's father William was a brother of Nellie Watson's mother Catherine, so Tom and Nellie[68]were first cousins and close friends. Tom's siblings were John, Willie, Jim (who had died aged four) and Peggy. Although a WW1 contemporary of Johnnie, and both from Cellardyke, these two Smith lads were not related at this time.

At the outbreak of WW1 Tom and his family lived at 6 Rodger Street, Cellardyke. Tom was a scholar at the Waid Academy, and was presented with the Dux medal for 1914–1915. He left the Waid and went to St Andrew's University, passing exams in Greek, Latin and Mathematics in March 1916.[69]

As Lieutenant Thomas Smith, he joined up. His "frontline service lasted no more than two months in total, yet was a constant cause of dread and anguish to his parents".[70]By October 1916 Tom had been badly wounded by shrapnel to his chest and he returned to hospital in Aberdeen, only being fit enough to return to active service in 1918.[71]He died aged 21 in October 1918. Sadly, William and Maggie's second son John died too, of illness, just after the war. The family never got over their loss, and it was still spoken of in hushed tones half a century later.

The back of this family photograph has these words:

1. John Smith, Peggy's brother, took flu, like a plague, and died after the war. (Peggy in front of John) 2. Auntie Nellie. 3. Tom Smith – Argyll and S. Highlanders. His captain was killed so Tom took over. In a battle he noticed that one of his men was caught on the barbed wire between the lines. His men said that the man was dead but Tom said that he must go to find out. So Tom went out and was shot by a sniper whilst attempting to cut the soldier free. He was taken as a Prisoner of War but died in France that same day.

L–R Back: John Smith (Bruce), Nellie Watson, Tom Smith. Child at front: Peggy Smith.

Peter Smith ('Poetry Peter') was the fisherman poet of Cellardyke. He was descended from a long line of fishermen and was born in George Street, Cellardyke, the youngest of a family of six. He was Nellie's[72] cousin once removed.

When war broke out in 1914, Peter, like many of his fellow fishermen, volunteered for active service. He was just forty years of age, but wasn't considered fit enough for active service. This was quite a surprise to Peter, a fisherman in a hazardous and physically demanding job, and he went back to the recruiting office on more than one occasion to see if he could be accepted.

Peter wrote two poems about the First World War. He chose to write in the Cellardyke dialect which was really more of a spoken language than a written one. My grandmother, Ailass,[73] told me how they had to "always speak in English" at school. The written language was always the English taught and used in schools, and there wasn't really a need to write in "oor ain tongue"[74] until writing poems or similar. This means that the spelling of the local dialect varied from person to person, and even the words used often varied from village to village. Peter's writing later inspired others to write in the Cellardyke dialect.[75]

My cousin Jimmy Corstorphine, in his edition of *A Selection of Poems by Peter Smith, the Fisherman Poet of Cellardyke*, comments:

> [The] poem called **The Fisherman** describes how in times of peace the important role played by the fisherman is often overlooked outside the confines of his own close-knit environment. In times of war, however, the fisherman becomes transformed into a provider of food supplies vital to the war effort. The poem goes on to remind the reader that, like the men fighting for their country in far off lands, the life of the fisherman is often fraught with danger.

Peter's poem 'This Awfu' War' builds into a prayer, asking God to keep a watchful eye over the soldiers and sailors caught up in the conflict. Like 'The Fisherman', it was written during WW1. This version was first published in 1951.

This Awfu' War

When first this awfu' war began
And we were socht to play the man,
Like mony mair, I up and ran
Tae dae my bit,
But look, I didna' ken till then
I wasna' fit.

I was abune the age nae doot,
Some teeth were rotten, ithers oot;
Then men were wantit, hale and stoot,
Without a flaw—
I couldna very well dispute
The Written Law.

Still, aye the cry was—Men, mair men,
Tae trawl or patrol on the main,
I tried it, ower and ower again,
But aye alas,
They met me, wi' the auld refrain,
You canna pass.

So, when oor laddies gae'd awa,
And joined the "Gallant Forty-Twa",
I prayed tae Him, wha rules ower a'
Tae look ower France,
Saying, "Faither if oor laddies fa'

Gie them a chance."

"Clap yer big haund ower a' their blots,
Frae Maidenkirk tae John o' Groats,
Frae the Seaforths tae the Royal Scots,
It disna' maitter,
Cam they frae palaces or cots
Or frae the gutter.

"Mind, tae, oor lads in Navy Blue,
Like ither folk, their thocht's o' You
At times may be baith scant and few
Yet guard them weel;
Their hearts are guid, and leal, and true,
Aye, true as steel.

"Watch ower them, in the summer breeze,
Watch ower them tae, when snaw sho'ers freeze,
Pilot them safe, thro' gey roch seas
As aince afore
You did it, by Lake Galilee's
Wild and stormy shore."

And you, wha sit at hame at ease
Roon' fires that toast yer very taes,
Mind them wha wear the khaki claes
As weel's the blue,
Whan 'tis decreed, that wars shall cease,
Gie them their due.

A World War One Black Watch soldier.

Appendix 3: The Family

After WW1, Johnnie continued his work as a marine engineer and married Helen (Nellie) Watson. They moved around with Johnnie's work, living in Helensburgh, Buckhaven and Burntisland, but always kept in close written contact with the family, visiting whenever they could.

In Cellardyke Nellie's brother Tom married Alice in 1923, and they had a daughter, named Joan. Nellie's sister Mary had married David, Johnnie's brother, in 1918, and they had a son, also called David.

A family gathering at 11 Shore Street, Cellardyke, 1950. L–R Standing: Joan Kingscott (née Watson), Ella Keay, Lizzie Bett, Nellie Smith (née Watson), Mary Smith (née Watson), Alice Watson (née Bett), Jessie Smith (née Reekie), Johnnie M. Smith. L–R Seated: William (Bert) Kingscott holding baby Alison Kingscott, David Smith holding toddler Dave Smith.

Paddling at Cellardyke. L–R: Bert, Alison, Uncle Johnnie and Dave.

Nellie and Johnnie at 16 East Forth Street, Cellardyke.

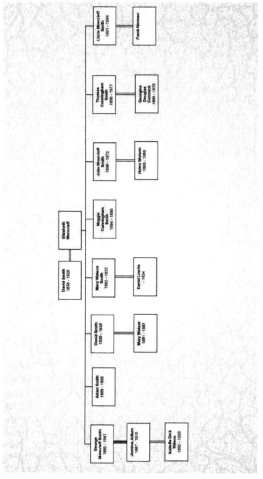

Johnnie's family tree, compiled and laid out by Dave Smith.

Census Insights

According to the 1891 census, Johnnie's parents, David Smith and Elizabeth (Moncrieff) had moved from their previous home in Jack's Building, Cowgate, (by 1888) to 76 Barclay Street,

Stonehaven, Aberdeenshire. Their eldest son George was six years old and another two sons, David and Adam, were born there.

David and Elizabeth's daughter Mary was born in 1892, by which time the family had moved to Anstruther. Mary was three years old when Johnnie was born. The family were living at 42 Shore Street, above a shop which is now the famous Anstruther Fish Bar!

The 1901 census reveals that at this time David and Elizabeth had moved just along the road to 33 Shore Street, Anstruther. David Smith, the head of the household, isn't shown on this census, so he must have been working away at that time. (Census date is night of 31st March – 1st April 1901) His wife Elizabeth is noted as 'wife of marine engineer'. George was aged 15, David was 11, Mary was eight, Johnnie was five and Tommie was three.

The 1911 census shows the family were still living at 33 Shore Street, Anstruther. Both David and Elizabeth are noted on the census this time and David was still a marine engineer. Johnnie was 15 and a general message boy. His older brother David was aged 21 and a 'marine stoker'.

Ten years later, aged 25 and having survived the war, Johnnie was living in Rosyth, as were the rest of his family, and it was from there that he married Nellie.

Timeline

1915

- Steam drifter *Craignoon* leaves Anstruther to go to Aberdeen, with a skeleton crew.
- Crew is issued with uniforms / remaining crew of Glasgow and Aberdeen men are collected.
- To Falmouth, Cornwall, getting "bunkers" (Johnnie's name for coal) on the way.
- To Gibraltar, with other steam drifters, getting "bunkers" in the middle of the Bay of Biscay!
- Two days in Gibraltar, across the Mediterranean, to take part in the Adriatic Campaign.
- To Brindisi, on the coast of the Adriatic Sea, their base for a year or so.
- Patrolling off coast of Albania, near the city of Durazzo, then back to Brindisi.
- Near Brindisi; a *Craignoon* disaster is avoided, but their flagship is lost to a mine.

1916

- January 8th 1916: Fraserburgh drifter *Morning Star*, 97 tonnes, is sunk by a mine off Brindisi.

- *Craignoon* transfers to Taranto. Duties involve "fishing for submarines" in the Straits of Otranto.
- June 1st 1916: Heavy firing. Fraserburgh drifter *Beneficient* is lost with no survivors.
- *Craignoon* alters course and heads for a mine. A piece of the mine ends up in the stokehold!

1917

- May 15th 1917: The *Craignoon* is sunk by gunfire, five or six miles west of Faro Island.
- The crew abandon ship. 14 drifters lost in what became known as the Battle of Otranto.
- The crews are rescued by an Austrian (enemy) ship, the *Novara*.
- En route to Cattero, lives are threatened, some lost, during a fight with three British cruisers.
- The 72 men, now POWs, are marched to an old Montenegrin prison fortress.
- May 21st 1917: POWs are transported for three days and nights to a prison in Graz, Austria.
- May 24th 1917: POWs arrive at Graz prison. No beds, starvation diet. Getting weaker by the day.
- June 15th 1917: POWs are put on display to show Britain 'starving', but British voices start to sing!
- June 21st 1917: POWs arrive at Deutsch Gabel, Bohemia, 3 miles from the German border.
- Autumn 1917: Letters from home and Red Cross food parcels arrive! Health is returning.

1918

- New uniforms arrive from London, with underclothes, boots and overcoats.
- Able-bodied men are sent to Laibach prison camp, mostly occupied by Russians and Italians.
- Johnnie is assigned as a group leader. Suffering and starvation, especially for the Russians.
- Johnnie decides to try to escape. Two tins of beef and a very long walk.
- Freedom continues for seven days, on foot and by train, heading for Trieste, Italy.
- A German general is surprised. Eventually Johnnie is returned to Deutsch Gabel.
- Johnnie greeted by James Wilson, then a punishment at Deutsch Gabel: 15 days in the cells.
- One day in camp, but the journey to Laibach, via Reichenburg, offers another escape.
- Johnnie is captured again, after just a few hours. He is put in "an empty cell in an empty camp".
- A further fifteen days' punishment, and this time six of the hours each day are to be in irons.
- Johnnie learns that he is to be sent to an officers' camp, near Vienna.
- Changing trains at Reichenburg railway station: A third escape is foiled. Guards more vigilant.
- Johnnie is made an orderly for an Aberdeen air force captain and an Edinburgh lieutenant.
- Return to the Austrian starvation diet: No more Red Cross food parcels.
- Walks for prisoners of good behaviour – and big juicy plums!

- Some old bread and stolen biscuits stave off starvation until good news of freedom!
- A two-day wait… and then a train to Trieste and a boat to Venice. Six days of quarantine.
- A journey on the wrong train near to the French front, where Germany is still fighting.
- By train to Paris, then on to Boulogne in an attempt to cross the channel
- On British soil at last: firstly to Devonport to good food and a new uniform.
- Granton Naval Base: refusing an order? Home leave and demobilisation.
- Looking back: Johnnie reflects on friendliness during his stay in as a POW in Austria.

Bibliography

Aswarm site. 'The Speakers: Austria WW1 Centenary', www.aswarm.com, 2014.

BBC History website, 2014. 'How did World War One Start?'

BBC News Magazine, 12th February 2014. 'World War One: 10 interpretations of who started WW1'

Cavallaro, G.V. *The Beginning of Futility: Diplomatic, Political, Military and Naval Events on the Austro-Italian Front in the First World War 1914-1917 Volume I*. Bloomington, IN: Xlibris, 2010.

Dittmar, F.J. & Colledge, J. J. *British Warships 1914–1919*. London: Ian Allan, 1972.

Dunion, K. *The Democracy of War: Anstruther and Cellardyke in the First World War* Anstruther: Kilrenny and Anstruther Burgh Collection, 2007. See also www.democracyofwar.co.uk

HistoryShelf website, www.historyshelf.org.uk

Forces War Records, www.forces-war-records.co.uk

Fraser, D. *Historic Fife*. Perth: Melven Press, 1982.

Gourlay, G. *Fisher Life: Or, theMemorials of Cellardyke and the Fife Coast.* Anstruther: Fife Herald, 1879.

Great War Forum website, www.1914-1918.invisionzone.com

The Great War 1914–1918 website, www.greatwar.co.uk

Halpern, P. G.The Battle of the Otranto Straits: Controlling the Gateway to the Adriatic in World War One. Bloomington, IN: Indiana University Press, 2004.

Humphries, A.E. 'John Bett RNR, WW1 Fisherman of Cellardyke', commemorative leaflet, 2015.

International Encyclopaedia of the First World War website, www.1914-1918-online.net

McKay, G. 'Report on the Raid by the Austrian Navy on the R.N. Drifters Operating the Otranto Boom Defence in the Adriatic Sea', on *Portsoy Past & Present* website

Naval History website, www.naval-history.net

Naval History website, 2009. 'British Naval Vessels Lost at Sea'

Phillips, R. 'The Otranto Barrage'
Rauchensteiner, M, *The First World War and The End of the Habsburg Monarchy 1914–1918.* Vienna: Boehlau Verlag, 2014.

Red Cross website, 'Food Parcels for Prisoners of War'

Smith, P. [Snr.] *The Herrin' and Other Poems.* Anstruther: C.S. Russell & Sons, circa 1951.

Smith, P. [Snr.] *A Selection of Poems by Peter Smith, the Fisherman Poet of Cellardyke,Compiled by James K. Corstorphine.* Leven: James K. Corstorphine, 2000.

Smith, P. *The Lammas Drave and The Winter Herrin': A History of the Herring Fishing from East Fife* Edinburgh: John Donald, 1985.

Smith, P. *The History of Steam and the East Fife Fishing Fleet.* Leven: James K. Corstorphine, 1998.

Smith P. *From The Sma' Lines And The Creels To The Seine Net And The Prawns: A Study Of The Inshore Fishing Industry Around The East Coast Of Fife From St. Andrews To Buckhaven.* Leven: James K. Corstorphine, 2001.

Stevenson, S. *Anstruther: A History.* Perth: John Donald Publishers, 1989. *Vox* website, '40 maps that explain World War I'

Watson, H. D. *Kilrenny and Cellardyke: 800 Years of History.* Edinburgh: John Donald, 1986.

Welch, M. *Anstruther Lifeboat Station: A History 1865–1985.*Kircaldy: Royal National Lifeboat Institution, 1985.

Wikipedia:
'Adriatic Campaign of WW1'

'Battle of the Strait of Otranto (1917)'
'Battle of Durazzo (1915)'
'Jablonné v Podještědí'

'Joseph Watt'
'List of prisoner-of-war camps in Germany'
'Ljubljana'
'Munitionettes'
'Otranto Barrage'
'Serbian Campaign of World War I'
'Serbian army's retreat through Albania'

Notes

Johnnie's World: Research Notes

[1] Dunion, Appendix 1

[2] Corstorphine, J. K., in introduction to Smith (2000), p. 14.

[3] This quote appears in the foreword to Smith's *The Herrin' and Other Poems*.

[4] Watson, p. 138

[5] Evidence suggests "then" is 1886, as he would have been 12 years old at this point.

[6] Watson, p. 183. Owners' names are in brackets.

[7] Watson, p. 116

[8] Much of the information in this paragraph comes from family notes, photographs and history as recorded by Joan Kingscott, (née Watson), Johnnie's niece by marriage.

[9] This detail was told to me by elderly relatives when I was a child.

[10] Gourlay, p. 104

[11] Gourlay, p. 131

[12] Gourlay, p. 135

[13] Fraser, p. 102

[14] *The Great War* website

[15] Smith (1998), p. 15

[16] *The Great War* website

[17] Dunion, p. 123

[18] Personal correspondence with H. Watson by email, 7/3/17.

[19] According to research by his grand-daughter, E. Stormonth.

[20] Information from the Scottish Fisheries Museum, Anstruther.

[21] Alex McKenzie's wife's comments as reported in a local newspaper. (Accessed via personal correspondence with E. Stormonth.)

[22] Alex McKenzie's wife's comments as reported in a local newspaper. (Accessed via personal correspondence with E. Stormonth.)

[23] Rauchensteiner

[24] *Wikipedia*, 'Battle of Durazzo (1915)'

[25] *Great War Forum* website

[26] *East of Fife Record,* 17th August 1916

[27] Smith (2001), p. 110

[28] Dunion, p. 146

[29] Dittmar and Colledge include the following information about the *Beneficient*:

Beneficient (FR 195) launched 1907, 80 tons, net minesweeper, sunk by gunfire off Saruichey Light Vessel, Adriatic Sea.

[30] McKay adds how the "drifters were made up in groups or sections numbered and lettered… with eight ships in a group."

[31] Information from the Scottish Fisheries Museum, Anstruther.

[32] *Wikipedia,* 'Serbian army's retreat through Albania'

[33] *BBC News Magazine* website

[34] *BBC History* website

[35] *Wikipedia,* 'Joseph Watt'

[36] Watson, p. 188

[37] Phillips' website

[38] *Wikipedia,* 'Otranto Barrage'

[39] Phillips' website

[40] Halpern, p. 163. Rear Admiral Alfredo Acton was the commanding officer of the Italian Scouting Division.

[41] Halpern, pp. 163–165

[42] McKay says: "Probably six or seven miles from where the Novara had dropped anchor and about one mile from the town of Castlenova."

[43] Watson, p. 187

[44] See *Aswarm* website, 'The Speakers'. The speakers were a multi-media installation in Graz, Austria, to commemorate the centenary of the start of WW1.

[45] McKay

[46] *International Encyclopaedia of the First World War,* 'Prisoners of War (Austria-Hungary)'

[47] *Red Cross* website

[48] Watson, p. 182 & p. 185

[49] *Wikipedia,* 'List of POW camps in Germany'

[50] *Wikipedia,* 'Jablonné v Podještědí'

[51] *Wikipedia,* 'Ljubljana'. In 1918, the city becomes part of the newly established Kingdom of Serbs, Croats and Slovenians.

[52] Reichenburg is now Liberec, in the Czech Republic.

[53] WW1 ended in Austria on 3rd November 1918, with the signing of the

Armistice of Villa Giusti, taking effect on 4th November 1918.

Appendix 1: The Royal Naval Reserve

[54] *Ancestry* message board, http://boards.ancestry.co.uk/thread.aspx?mv=flat&m=167&
ics.Military.uk.rn

[55] *Great War Forum* message board: http://1914-1918.invisionzone.com/fo-
rums/index.php?/topic/70223-what-doests-mean-in-the-rn/

Appendix 2: Uncle Johnnie and Wartime Contemporaries

[56] Tragically, Mary and David died whilst missionaries in Africa.

[57] Lists of names and dates copied by Nellie from the family bible.

[58] *Wikipedia*, 'Munitionettes'

[59] Kingscott, J.B. (née Watson), family notes.

[60] 1911 census via Harry Watson

[61] A medal presented to the top pupil in the class.

[62] Tom and Alice's marriage certificate (25/06/1923) gives Tom's occupation as "Master Cabinetmaker".

[63] Tom survived the war but died in 1933, when Joan was seven years old.

[64] Army Form Z.18, 'Certificate of Employment During The War'. Signed: *N. Noble, Lieutenant.*

[65] Dunion, p. 10

[66] In Kilrenny Churchyard, John Bett has a war grave plus a memorial stone in the shape of a scroll, reading:
"A Token of Esteem from his Comrades".

[67] Dunion, p. 23

[68] See Helen Smith.

[69] Dunion, p. 102

[70] Dunion, p. 101

[71] Dunion, p. 101

[72] See Helen Smith.

[73] See Alice Bett.

[74] See *Scottish National Dictionary*, www.dsl.ac.uk

[75] See Nellie's *Memories and Reflections: An East Neuk Anthology* (1995), which includes a poem dedicated to Peter.

Printed in Great Britain
by Amazon

Copyright Notice

Strolling Around Ljubljana by Irene Reid

ISBN: 9781549610622

Get Ready

The Ljubljana Card

City cards are always worth investigating as they can save you both money and time. If you plan to visit the castle, take boat ride, and pop into some of the museums then it's probably worthwhile buying. You can buy the Ljubljana card either at the tourist office in Preseren trg, or online at:

https://www.visitljubljana.com/en/visitors/ljubljana-card/

The Walks

There are four walks around Ljubljana.

Walks 1 and 2 will take you up and down the riverbanks where you will see the most famous and popular sights.

Walk 3 will take you away from the riverbank to see the Slovenian Parliament and into the Museum Quarter.

Walk 4 will take you into two of Ljubliana's oldest suburbs where you can see its Roman heritage.

Potted History

Archaeologists tell us that people started to arrive in the Ljubljana arca in the Stone Age. In fact the oldest known musical instrument in the world is a flute made from bone which was found in Slovenia and made by Neanderthal man; it's 60,000 years old.

Just as intriguing is the oldest wheel in the world which was found in the marshes around Ljubljana – from 3250 BC.

Much later, around 2000 BC, the people began to build houses on stilts in the marshes and lakes which were sprinkled all around this area – which was very handy for a bit of fishing. Those people are today called The Pile Dwellers.

The Romans arrived as they conquered their way across Europe, and built the first permanent buildings for their legionnaires. They called their settlement Emona, and Ljubljana has some ruins and remnants from Roman times which you will see on all the walks.

After the Roman Empire had fallen little Emona soldiered on, and its name gradually changed to Aemona. The Huns, the Lombards, and the Goths all crisscrossed Europe in the next couple of centuries, and they all stopped at Aemona to sack it and then move on. Finally in the 6th century the Slovenians turned up having fled from the Magyars in modern day Hungary, and they decided to stay.

The little town grew but eventually fell under the rule of its powerful northern neighbour the Austo-Hungarian Empire. Like most of Europe the rich were very, very rich and the poor were very, very poor. In 1515 the peasants revolted across Slovenia demanding more rights. The revolt was finally crushed after just 12 days by an army of mercenaries hired by the Holy Roman Empire. Despite this, by the end of the sixteenth century, the Slovenian people began to see themselves as a nation with their own language and culture.

4

Napoleon invaded in 1809, and he made Ljubljana the capital of what he called the Illyrian Provinces. Of course when Napoleon fell so did the Illyrian Provinces, which were once again gobbled up by the surrounding powers.

World War I did not have any major impact on the city, but at its end in 1918 the State of Slovenes, Croats, and Serbs was proclaimed in Ljubljana, and it eventually became Yugoslavia.

World War II was a very different story. At the start of World War II Yugoslavia was split up between the Axis powers. Ljubljana was grabbed by Italy whilst the rest of Slovenia fell to Germany and Hungary. The Italians had long wanted to get their hands on Slovenia. Mussolini is quoted as saying in 1920:

"When dealing with such a race as Slavic - inferior and barbarian - we must not pursue the carrot, but the stick policy. We should not be afraid of new victims. The Italian border should run across the Brenner Pass, Monte Nevoso, and the Dinaric Alps. I would say we can easily sacrifice 500,000 barbaric Slavs for 50,000 Italians."

The Italians didn't trust the Slovenians at all, so they surrounded Ljubljana with thirty kilometers of barbed wire effectively cutting it off from the world. It happened overnight on Feb 24 1942, and the barbed wire was soon followed by bunkers and checkpoints. Of course this made the people behind the barbed wire hate the Italians even more, and resistance grew

The barbed wire stayed for over 3 years until the war ended, and Slovenia disappeared into the conglomerate of communist Yugoslavia. Every year Ljubljana's people walk around "The Trail of Remembrance and Comradeship" which marks where the barbed wire ran.

Once the Iron Curtain fell, Slovenia grasped its chance for independence, broke free of Yugoslavia, and joined the European Community.

The Maps

There are maps sprinkled all through the walks to help you find your way. If you need to check where you are at any point during a walk, always flip back to find the map you need.

The Stars

Apart from Mrs Melania Trump, naming famous Slovenians is probably quite a hard task. One you will become very familiar with as you explore is Joze Plecnik. He came from Ljubljana and was the son of a carpenter. At first he seemed to be following in his father's footsteps, but then he diverted to architecture and studied in Vienna. He was asked to design buildings in Vienna, Belgrade, and Prague but he finally came home to Ljubljana.

He became the most influential architect in Slovenia in modern times, and he was responsible for many of the sights you will see as you explore. In fact Ljubljana is affectionately known as Plecnik's Ljubljana. He designed the library, the cemetery, the market, reworked the riverbanks, and redesigned central Ljubljana – the list goes on and on. Apparently his plan was to model central Ljubljana on ancient Athens.

Walk 1 – The Castle and Preseren trg

This walk starts in Preseren trg.

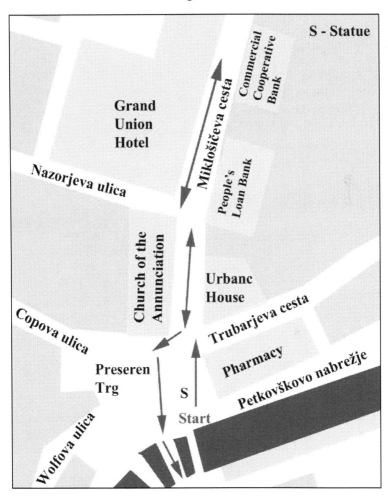

Preseren trg

This is one of Ljubljana's most popular squares, usually buzzing with people meeting and shopping. Try to fit in a visit in the evening if you get the chance; life slows down, and the locals meander rather than race to their next destination.

Preseren trg used to be just a crossroads but was converted into a square in the nineteenth century. It was redesigned after the huge 1895 earthquake when a lot of the old buildings were flattened and replaced by the palaces and mansions you see now. There was a proposal quite recently to add a fountain to the square but oddly the people said no!

France Preseren

The bronze statue which stands at one side of the square is one of Slovenia's greatest poets, France Preseren – the square is named after him. One of his poems was made part of the National Anthem.

A statue was proposed by students and scholars, and the idea was taken up by the then Mayor of Ljubljana. A competition was announced, and this is the winning design. Its construction was financed by donations from the public and unveiled in 1905 in front of 20,000 people.

Preseren is holding a book of his poems, and he is looking towards a building on Wolfova Street, where it's said he first saw Julija Primic looking out of a nearby window.

She was the love of his life. Sadly Julija was from a wealthy family and Preseren was from the peasant class, so her family would not even consider him a worthy match. Preseren wrote many poems to Julija, and his most famous work, "Wreath of Sonnets" was dedicated to her. It was all for nothing though as Julija married a wealthy man and was forever out of Preseren's reach.

Above Preseren you can see the Muse of Poetry, who caused outrage at first because she is not wearing much. Opinion was divided - the church wanted her removed and replaced with a much more modest statue, which prompted the local press to mock the church. Preseren's muse survived the disapproval, but it's said that the trees in front of the nearby pink church were put there to block worshipers' views of the muse's breasts.

Central Pharmacy

Just behind the statue stands Ljubljana's oldest pharmacy in a rather grand building. The building also housed a café called Preseren's Café – it survived until World War II and it's a shame it has not been restored.

Face the pharmacy and the building on the left is the Urbanc House

Urbanc House

This is a lovely Art Nouveau store which was built by Feliks Urbanc. Nowadays it's known as the Galerija Emporium.

When it was originally built the owner's name was emblazoned on the outside of the building, but in 1946 it was registered as property of the "Federal People's Republic of Yugoslavia", the owner's name was obliterated, and the store was rechristened as CentroMerurk. It was in a sorry state after decades of neglect while Slovenia languished behind the iron curtain.

When the iron curtain fell Urbanc's grandsons took the store over, and it has been lovingly restored. Right at the top is Mercury watching over the square, and if you have a good camera lens you might be able to see that at Mercury's feet is the head of Feliks Urbanc himself.

Go inside to see the stunningly lovely staircase and have a look around. Spot the statue which represents "craft"

Once back outside turn right into Miklošičeva cesta and walk past the pink church on your left.

Miklošičeva cesta

You will pass Nazorjeva ulica on your left. The next building on your left is the Grand Hotel Union, which was one of the greatest hotels in southeastern Europe. It has had many famous visitors, Orson Welles, Hilary and Bill Clinton, the Dalai Lama, and The United Kingdom's Queen Elizabeth. It has a lovely Art Nouveau doorway – and if you venture inside you could visit the Grand Union Café, which is known for its excellent teas and coffees.

Just opposite the hotel at number 4 is the cream, blue and red People's Loan Bank. The three colours used represent the Slovenian flag which you can usually see outside the building. The building also has a lovely iron balcony railing, and right at the top are two ladies representing Industry (holding what's supposed to be a beehive full of busy bees) and wealth (holding a purse).

The eye-catching Commercial Cooperative Bank is at number 8, a bit further up the street. Inside is even more colourful and ornate than the outside. The bank was designed by Ivan Vurnik, and his wife who was also a designer planned the beautiful decorations inside and outside. Unfortunately it's not open to the public.

Face the bank and turn right to make your way back to Preseren trg, again passing the pink Church of the Annunciation on your right. Walk around to the front of the church.

The Church of the Annunciation

This church is a colourful salmon pink colour these days. It was originally bright red to symbolise the Franciscan monks who built it, but over the years it has faded to a gentler hue.

Outside and right at the top you can see The Lady of Loretto, a copper statue which replaced a much older wooden Black Madonna. You need to stand well back to see her properly. She stands above a triple stairway – you will find that they like things in triplicate in Ljubljana.

Go inside. The church was badly damaged in the 1895 earthquake, and the frescoes you see on the ceiling are from last century to rectify the damage. If you look to the left of the altar you can see a glass coffin with what is said to be the remains of Saint Deodatus in full view – you can make your own mind up on how authentic it looks!

The altar is worth a look. It was sculpted by a famous Italian sculptor, Francesco Robba, who visited Ljubljana and fell in love with a local girl. So he stayed in town and applied his skills to Ljubljana's churches.

The Triple Bridge

Back on the riverside is one of Ljubljana's most famous sights, The Triple Bridge. Originally there was just one bridge, but traffic was growing rapidly so Plecnik designed the triple bridge by adding

12

two side pedestrian bridges as well as the pretty lamps and stonework. Plecnik's plan was to make this bit of Ljubljana look like Venice.

This area used to be just a huge knot of traffic, but in 2007 the pedestrian won and traffic was turned out – so you can stroll over one bridge span and return on another.

If you cross on one of the side bridges you can look over to see the stairways giving access to the river banks. On the other side of the river turn round to get a great view of Preseren trg.

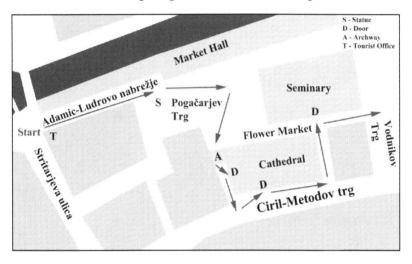

If you need the tourist office it's just on the corner of Adamič-Lundrovo nabrežje and Stritarjeva ulica.

Now face away from the bridge and turn left along Adamič-Lundrovo nabrežje to enjoy Plecnik's Market Hall.

Plecnik's Market Hall

This lovely building which follows the curve of the riverside was designed by Plecnik, and you can see his plan to replicate Athens coming to fruition with columns and arcades. The Market Hall is on two floors with stalls selling all sorts of meats, cheeses, and pastries.

The road will open out into a wide square called Pogačarjev trg.

Spot the odd cone shaped monument to Plecnik on your right near the entrance to the square – it was erected in 1993. Apparently Plecnik designed a new Parliament Building in the same shape to stand on Vodnikov trg which you will reach soon, but sadly it was never built. It would have certainly been eye-catching. Have a look at any spare change you have, if you find a 2007 Slovenian Euro coin, you can see what Plecnik planned.

Walk into the middle of the square and face away from the river. You will see the back of the cathedral in front of you.

Go through the double archway ahead of you. Walk up the side of the Cathedral and you will see a Cathedral side door on your left,

St Nicholas Cathedral

The Cathedral is dedicated to Saint Nicholas, the patron saint of fishermen and boatmen. It might seem odd that Ljubljana had so many fishermen as it lies quite a way from any open water, but there is access to the Black Sea via the Ljubljanica river, the Sava river, and finally the Danube. Also don't forget that before they drained the surrounding land, Ljubljana lay in the midst of marshes. The fishermen and boatmen were a very important guild in old Ljubljana, and they had a church on this site before the Cathedral was built.

Just before the visit of Pope John Paul II, two of the cathedral doors were replaced with magnificent bronze doors. The door you

14

see at the side celebrates the history of Christianity in Ljubljana watched over by Slovenian bishops and Pope John Paul II.

Continue along the side of the cathedral and turn left into Ciril-Metodov trg to reach the front of the Cathedral and the Holy Door. You will see a line of Ljubljana bishops looking over what I assume is Jesus – it's a bit ghoulish.

The Cathedral you see today is not the original. The ancient building which first stood here was in a sorry state after the earthquakes, so rather than trying to shore it up, they decided to knock it down and build a new one. Very little was kept of the original, but if you stand back from the door and look left, you will see an alcove which holds a little pieta from the 15th century which was saved.

Go inside for a blast of pink marble, glimmering gilt, and a swathe of colourful frescoes. You can see that the cathedral now has a dome, but when the cathedral was being built Ljubljana ran out of money. So for many years there was a false ceiling where the dome is now, with a dome painted on it instead. If you look up to the top of the columns supporting the dome you can see several Coats of Arms. No-one really knows why they are there, but the assumption is that they commemorate the families who helped finance the dome's construction.

The side pulpits are quite unusual as they each have an organ directly above them.

When you exit the cathedral turn left. Spot the sundial on the front of the cathedral as you walk along.

Seminary

When you reach the end of the Cathedral look left to see a splendid door with two giant figures on either side. Walk down to get a closer look. This is the Seminary and like a lot of interesting buildings in Ljubljana you can't actually get in to see its priceless library except by arranged tour.

If it's a Saturday you will see a lovely flower market running along the back of the Cathedral – the stalls are run by locals selling flowers from their own gardens or allotments.

Face the Seminary door and turn right to walk into Vodnikov trg.

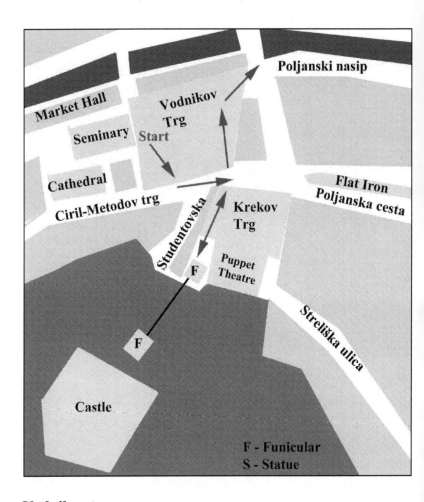

Vodnikov trg

This square came into being after a huge earthquake in 1895 which shook most of the old town apart. A large monastery which stood here fell down so the cleared space was turned into a market square. You will probably find the Central Market in full swing so take a few minutes to have a look around – and perhaps make a purchase. There are stalls selling all sorts of fruits, vegetables, and flowers, often from the sellers' allotments and only harvested that morning. The best market day is Saturday, but it is closed on Sundays.

The square was named after a Slovenian poet, Valentin Vodnik – you will find the Slovenes are very fond of naming their squares after favourite poets. He actually started as a priest and preached in various parts of Slovenia, but he eventually returned to Ljubljana and became part of the intellectual circle of Ziga Zois – remember that name as you will come across it later. Vodnik wrote his poems in Slovenian and they were very patriotic, extolling Slovenia's language and heritage. He was also the editor of the very first Slovenian newspaper, the Lublanske News. He stands on the side of the square at the bottom of the castle hill.

You have a choice on how you tackle Castle hill.

The path is quite rough in some places, so if you decide to use it take care. Also if you visit in the evening remember to take a torch! If you feel fit and able, face the same way as Vodnik and walk straight ahead onto Študentovska ulica - it will take you onto a woody path and up the hill to the castle.

For the less energetic, face the same way as Vodnik but then turn left to walk into smaller Kreko trg.

Puppet Theatre

The large building running along the far end of the square is the Ljubjana Puppet theatre, and it's not just for children. It started at the start of last century and became the leading puppet theatre in the then Yugoslavia.

The puppeteers started using traditional marionettes but expanded to use very modern technology as well. Popular shows are Spotty the Ball and Twinkle Sleepyhead for children, to Doctor Faustus for the grown-ups.

If you are intrigued you can find out what is on either at the box office or here

http://www.lgl.si/en/

If you happen to be in the square on the hour you can at least watch the puppet clock in action. It was installed in 1992 and shows us a scene from the first puppet show put on when the theatre re-opened in in 1983.

It's a traditional Slovenian folk tale called "Martin Krpan from Vrh". Krpan was a peasant from the little Slovenian town of Vrh. He was incredibly strong and he became a hero when he fought and killed an evil giant called Brdavs who had murdered the Emperor's son. The horse is his little mare which he rode into battle on.

To the right of the theatre is the entrance to the funicular.

Funicular

It was Mayor Hribar who first put the idea to the Hapsburg rulers back at the end of the 19th century.

> "Because the view from the spaces in question (of the Ljubljana Castle) are charmingly beautiful, and because it would be good to make use of the current shady courtyard, if only we built an elevator with which one could reach the top for a mere ten kreutzers or less, it would no doubt attract many visitors, particularly on summer evenings."

They didn't take the idea up and it was not until 2006 that the Funicular was built. The Mayor had the right idea because by 2014 it had carried two million passengers up to the castle. For those interested in the figures, it has a maximum speed of 3 meters per second and takes one minute from top to bottom – a lot faster than walking!

You can buy your tickets online which will save a bit of money and time. Remember if you have chosen to buy the Ljubljana card it includes a ride on the funicular and a visit to the castle.

http://www.ljubljanskigrad.si/en/visit-us/opening-hours-and-prices/

Whichever way you tackle the hill, once at the top make your way to the castle entrance.

The Castle

If you need to defend yourself, building a castle on a hill is always a good idea. Ljubljana was always in danger from a Turkish invasion, so the castle you see today is the last in a long line of defensive buildings which were placed here. The castle was built by the Habsburgs, the family who ruled huge swathes of Europe from the fourteenth century onwards.

When Napoleon arrived in the eighteenth century he was seen by many as a liberator from the autocratic rule of the Hapsburgs – he gave the people freedom and education. That lasted only as long as Napoleon did, and when he fell the Hapsburgs returned, and this time they used their castle as a prison.

It was still a prison until World War II when the Germans marched in. It was left in a poor condition and only in the 1970's did Ljubljana start to restore it. Today it's a busy tourist attraction.

There is a twenty minute video which will give you a good background to Ljubljana which is worth sitting through. There is also a tower which can be climbed for the best views. In the sixteenth century the original Piper's Tower stood in the same spot. Every morning and evening, the opening and closing of the city gates was accompanied by music played by musicians from the top of the tower.

The castle is also a popular place for weddings so if you visit on a Saturday you can enjoy a procession of wedding dresses.

When you have had enough take the funicular back downhill to make sure you get back to Krekov trg. There are also several footpaths down, but if you decide to walk you may find yourself some distance from Krekov trg where the walk continues.

Peglezen

Once down walk straight ahead to cross Krekov trg. As you do, glance right along Polinjanska cesta to see Plecnik's flat-iron building fronted by its colourful flagpole. Peglezen is Slovenian for flatiron - it's a little smaller than New York's Flatiron skyscraper and was build 23 years later in 1925. The flagpole you see was removed during World War II but restored in 1989.

Return to the larger neighbouring square Vodnikov trg, and cross it diagonally right to reach the Dragon Bridge.

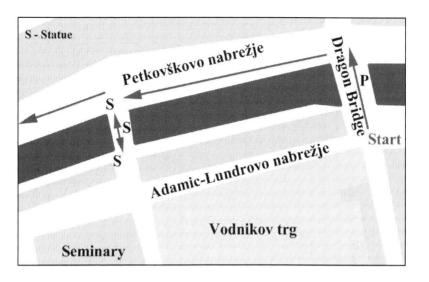

Dragon Bridge

Before the 1895 earthquake an old wooden bridge crossed the river here. When it collapsed Ljubljana decided to build a new bridge, and the town wanted something with style. The city planners commissioned a bridge design from a Viennese firm, and the reinforced concrete bridge which was built was revolutionary in its time. It is one of Europe's earliest reinforced concrete bridges, and is protected as a "Technical Monument".

The bridge was then decorated with four large snarling copper dragons and 16 smaller dragons were sprinkled along the balustrade. It was completed in 1907 and dedicated to Franz Joseph I of the Hapsburg Dynasty, but it was always called the Dragon Bridge.

Hribar

There is a plaque hallway across honouring Ivan Hribar who was Mayor of Ljubljana when the bridge was built. He was Ljubljana's most respected mayor who strove to improve his city and make his people see themselves as a nation. He was the driving force behind a lot of the lovely buildings you have seen on your exploration of Ljubljana. He committed suicide when Slovenia was invaded by Italy in 1941 at the age of ninety. He jumped into the Ljubljanica wrapped in the flag of Yugoslavia, and left behind a note with a verse from one of Preseren's poems:

> Less fearful the long night of life's denial
> Than living 'neath the sun in subjugation!

Dragons

The city's coat of arms includes a Dragon and you might wonder why. As usual there is a legend connecting the city with the heroes of ancient time. When Jason and his Argonauts were on the run after pinching the Golden Fleece, they sailed up the Danube to escape their pursuers and ended up sailing into the Ljubljanica. They stopped for a while to gather their strength before the journey home to Greece, and while there they came across a monstrous dragon that Jason finally slew after a long battle.

Watch out as you cross, as the legend tells us that if a virgin crosses the bridge the dragons wag their tails.

Once on the other side of the river turn left into Petkovškovo nabrežje to explore the riverfront. This area is full of restaurants so you might find somewhere which appeals for lunch or an evening meal. As you stroll along the riverside look back to the Dragon Bridge – in the middle you can see the golden plaque which commemorates Emperor Franz Josef I. You might also be able to see the delicate leaves carved into the balustrade on the river side – if you can't get close enough you will definitely see them on your boat trip.

You will eventually reach the next bridge.

Butcher's Bridge

The narrow butcher's bridge was built for pedestrians only, and it's a bit controversial. It is relatively modern (2010), and not everyone appreciated the statues and the design – so walk over and see for yourself. You can walk on the glass walkways and see the river beneath you.

First you meet poor old Prometheus who has his liver eaten every day by an eagle in punishment for giving the secret of fire to mankind – his pesky liver regrows every night. Next up is The Satyr who is startled by the serpent he is about to wrestle. Finally on the other side, Adam and Eve have just left Eden in shame.

It has to be said that they wouldn't shine if placed next to any of the classical statues like Florence's David – but it's all a matter of taste.

You will probably also have noticed the padlocks as you walked across the bridge, the modern symbol of eternal love. You will also see some skulls, toads, and fossils sprinkled along the sides of the bridge. Some of the lovers have even attached their padlocks to the toads. Less romantically, it's only a matter of time before the padlocks are snapped open and removed.

Having examined the statues, cross the bridge again and turn left onto Petkovškovo nabrežje again to continue along the riverside. You get the best view of the Market Hall from this side of the river.

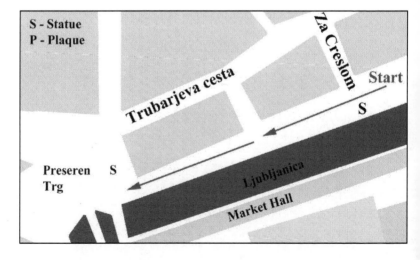

This side of the river is a lovely spot for a cool drink – if you can find a table. Not too far along you will reach a little viewing platform guarded by a dog which seems to be offering a paw to passers-by. It was sculpted by the same artist who did the statues on the Butcher's Bridge.

Continue along the riverside until you return to Preseren trg where Walk 1 ends.

Boat Trip

Make sure you fit a boat trip into your schedule, as seeing the city glide past on the river is very pleasant. There are many companies which all do essentially the same trip. Remember that the Ljubljana Card includes a boat trip – so check your information leaflet for its departure point and timetable.

Walk 2 – The library and the Old Town

This walk also starts in Preseren trg.

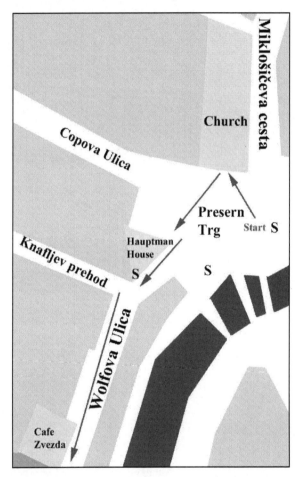

Hauptman House

Stand in front of Preseren's statue and face the same way as Preseren. The lovely building directly in front of you is the

Hauptman House, which somehow managed to survive the earthquake without any damage. It was renovated shortly after the earthquake and decorated with ceramic tiles in greens, blues, and reds – it is probably the prettiest building on the square. Its nickname is The Little Skyscraper.

Just in front of the Hauptman House you will find a bronze model of Ljubljana; you can try to spot where your hotel is.

Wolfova Street

Take a walk down Wolfova Street on the left of Hauptman House.

Not too far along at number 4 you can see a little statue of Julija looking out of her bedroom window. She was the unrequited love of France Preseren who you read about on Walk 1.

Continue along Wolfova Street. You will come to Café Zvezda on your right at number 14. It is one of the best patisseries in town if coffee and cake is needed.

Continue and you will walk into Kongresni trg.

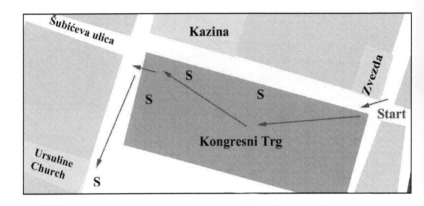

Kongresni trg

This square used to hold a Capuchin monastery, but it was demolished and replaced with Kongresni trg when the 1821 Congress of the Holy Alliance took place here. The square was embellished and prettified for the event.

The Congress was basically an emergency meeting convened by Europe's Royal Families to discuss what was to be done about the peasant uprisings, and even worse, the middle classes who were getting entirely too confident and interfering. They basically agreed to help each other stamp out any rebellions on the pretext of maintaining peace. However times were changing - rebellions and revolutions were breaking out all over Europe.

It was here that independence from the Austro-Hungarian Empire was first declared in 1918 and the fledgling Yugoslavia came into being. Ironically it was also here that the first demonstration against Yugoslav rule was held in 1988 – leading to the declaration of independence in 1991. President Clinton was the first US President to visit Slovenia, and he made a speech on Kongresni trg in 1999. It is a hugely symbolic square to the people of Ljubljana.

You can see that it has a garden area on the right and a paved area on the left. In fact the paved area was a car park at one time, but the cars have been ejected making it a much nicer place to visit.

Walk through the green garden towards the far end of the square. As you do you will pass a large anchor on your right – it was put there to commemorate the annexation of the Primorje area by Slovenia giving vital access to the Mediterranean and stopping Italian expansion into the region.

On you right near the end of the square you will see the pink Kazina House.

Kazina House

This lovely palace was built as a venue for balls and social gatherings, and it has one of Ljubljana's most remarkable interiors, but again you can't get inside to see it! Love-struck France Prešeren met Julija at a ball held here. During World War II the German occupying forces used it as their headquarters.

Just outside Kazina House is a statue of a little child. It is a Plecnik memorial to the women of Ljubljana who protested against the imprisonment of Slovenian men during the Italian occupation in WWII.

Roman Patrician

At the end of the park you will find a golden statue of a Roman patrician which was dug up in Ljubljana in the nineteenth century – the original is in the National Museum which you might have just visited. Turn left to reach the Ursuline Church.

Ursuline Church of the Holy Trinity

This much loved church with its six towering columns was put on the Slovenian banknotes when Slovenia became independent in 1991 – and it stayed there until the Euro arrived in 2007. It was originally financed by a wealthy merchant, Schellenburg, in the eighteenth century, and at that time had a garden. However the garden has not survived. Plecnik was responsible for the finishing touch of the ornate balustrade at the main door.

The entrance is to the right of the main door, so if it's open go in to see the main altar which Robba sculpted from multi-coloured African marble.

Holy Trinity column

The first Trinity statue which was erected in front of the church was put up as a thank-you to God for mostly sparing Ljubljana from the Black Death. It was a wooden column, and at some point the decision was taken to replace it with a stone column. The statues at the top were sculpted by Robba – well actually they are copies as the originals are now safely in the City Museum.

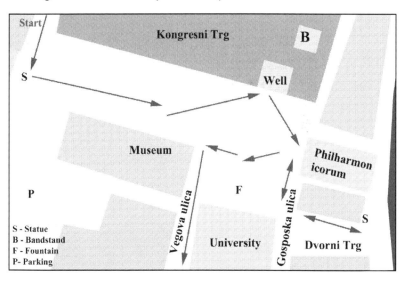

Walk back down the square on the paved area, and as you approach the end you will see the handsome Academia

Philharmonicorum in front of you. You also get a lovely view of the castle high on its hill.

Museum of illusion

As you walk down the square you will reach number 13 on your right which houses the Museum of Illusion. It's not really a museum, but an interactive display of optical illusions, and it's quite fun if you need a break from sight-seeing, or perhaps to get out of the rain.

Academia Philharmonicorum

Right at the bottom of the square is the Philharmonicorum which is easy to spot as it proclaims its identity across the top. This is where the Slovenian Philharmonic Orchestra started in 1701, and over the years it has had many illustrious members, Haydn, Beethoven, Mozart, Paganini, Brahms, and Mahler – although Mahler is the only one to have worked there. In fact being conductor at the Academia was his first job.

The building has had its disasters – it burned down in 1887 and had to be rebuilt. It was then shaken by the earthquake and had to be restored again. It is beautiful inside but unfortunately you can only see it if you actually attend a concert. You could find out if there is a concert you would be interested in here:

http://en.filharmonija.si/

Bandstand

Facing the Philharmonicorum you will see a little bandstand. Long ago concerts were played here but now there is far too much noise from traffic so it stands forlorn and unused.

Roman Well

Just in front of the Philharmonicorum are some steps. Descend the steps and you will find evidence of Ljubljana's roman past - an old Roman Well.

Mahler

Before moving on turn left into Dvorni trg and walk down to the riverside. Look to your left and you will find a statue of Mahler, and just beyond him you can see the unusual undulating rear of the Philharmonicorum.

Now return up the steps to Kongresni trg and stand with the Academia Philharmonicorum on your left - the lovely administration centre of the University is right in front of you.

University Building

This is where each year's new students are registered. The fountain in front of the lovely University Building is called Europa and it celebrates the EU recognition of Slovenia in 1992. The balcony is where Tito made a speech in 1945.

Tito was of course the architect and dictator of communist Yugoslavia. However there were as many tensions in the communist world as the democratic world, and Stalin and Tito did not see eye to eye on many things. At one point Yugoslavia almost went to war with the rest of the Communist world with soldiers massing on both sides of the Yugoslavian border. War was avoided but Yugoslavia was an outcast in the communist world. Stalin tried to have him assassinated but failed, and he famously told Stalin:

> *"Stop sending people to kill me. We've already captured five of them, one of them with a bomb and another with a rifle. If you don't stop sending killers, I'll send one to Moscow, and I won't have to send a second."*

He died in 1980 in Ljubljana, and his funeral was one of the biggest the world had seen with royalty and statesmen from all over the world attending. The New York Times wrote:

> Tito sought to improve life. Unlike others who rose to power on the communist wave after WWII, Tito did not long demand that his people suffer for a distant vision of a better life. After an initial Soviet-influenced bleak period, Tito moved toward radical improvement of life in the country. Yugoslavia gradually became a bright spot amid the general grayness of Eastern Europe.

Walk along Vegova ulica which is to the right of the University Building.

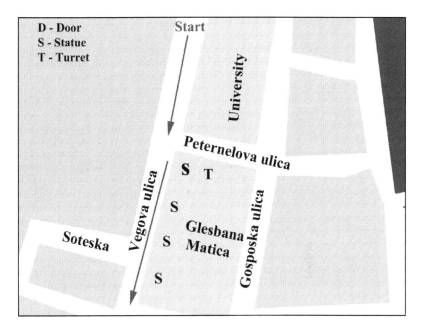

Legend:
D - Door
S - Statue
T - Turret

Start

University

Peternelova ulica

Vegova ulica

Soteska

Glesbana Matica

Gosposka ulica

Roman Legacy

Once past The University Building you will see a building on your left which has a distinctive turret. Its foundations follow the line of a Roman gatehouse and turret which guarded Emona's eastern wall.

A little further on is the Glesbana Matica.

Glesbana Matica

The translation is great – the Music Nut. This is a society which was originally established to promote and preserve Slovenian music. These days it concentrates on publishing sheet music and selling CDs of Slovenian music.

The front of the Music Nut is lined with pedestals, each one bearing the head of a Slovenian composer. There is even a Serb and

Croatian composer in the line-up. However unless you are very knowledgeable you probably won't have heard of any of them.

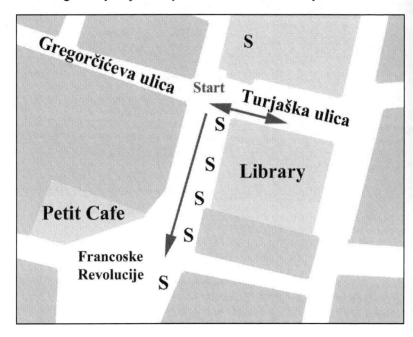

Once past the Glesbana Matica you will reach Turjaška ulica, and across it on your left you can see one of Ljubljana's most famous buildings, the National Library.

Library

It's the variegated building with red bricks interspersed with grey granite on the left. This is Jože Plecnik's masterpiece. It sits right at the edge of medieval Ljubljana. It was built between 1936 and 1941, which is surprising as that was when Europe was destroying so much during World War II. In fact it was damaged during the war when a plane crashed into the reading room in 1944 - but fortunately it was a small plane and the library survived.

It holds over 1.3 million books and storage is now a major problem.

Turn left down Turjaška ulica and you will find the main door of the library – which has splendid horsehead door-handles. Before you go in, stand back and look up at the windows on the top floor – they are supposed to represent books with the spine of the books facing outwards.

Now go in if it's open. You will find yourself in gloom with an impressive black marble stairway rising above you. Climb the steps to be surrounded by black marble columns – with the reading room straight ahead of you – but it is guarded and you can't go any further. The architect said

"From the twilight of ignorance
to the light of knowledge and enlightenment".

The main reading room is only accessible by a tour in July and August – outside that only students are allowed in. You could descend to the basement and pop into the café to mingle with the students over a coffee.

When you exit the library turn left to return to Vegova ulica. Turn left again into Vegova ulica to walk along the front of the library. As mentioned in the potted history, Ljubljana started as a Roman town, and part of the Roman town wall ran alongside the library where you are now. Plecnik decided to honour the city's ancient history by lining the route of the old wall with statues of famous Slovenians – although it has to be admitted you will probably not have heard of them.

At the end is a statue of the poet Simon Gregorčič. You have now reached Trg Francoske Revolucije – French Revolution Square.

Illyrian Monument

When Napoleon stretched his empire along the Adriatic, he named the region the Illyrian Provinces and decided to make Ljubljana the capital. This monument celebrates that glorious moment of importance, as Slovenia had been ruled by the Austrian Hapsburg Empire up till then. Unlike many of the countries invaded by Napoleon, Slovenia was ambivalent about the French invasion and were happy to embrace the French principles of equality, liberty, and fraternity.

There are two golden heads on the column - one is Napoleon and the other represents Illyria. Below Napoleon is a poem penned by Vodnik in praise of Napoleon - you saw Vodnik's statue on walk one in Vodnik trg. At the top is the old coat of arms of Slovenia. This is the only statue to Napoleon outside of France as most countries did not appreciate being invaded.

Le petit café – Caffeine stop

If you feel the need for a coffee at this point, you could consider the bohemian Le Petit Café near the Illyrian Monument.

When you are ready to move on, return to the Illyrian Monument.

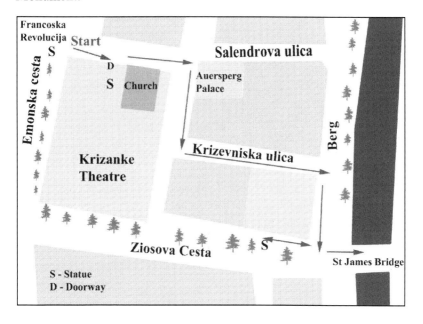

Face Napoleon and turn left to walk towards a faded pink church at the end of the street on your right. Just before the church you will see a gateway into a lovely entrance courtyard of the Krizanke Theatre.

Krizanke Church and Theatre

The entire square which the church is part of, was once a Monastery built in the thirteenth century by the Order of Teutonic Knights.

The Knights were established in Europe in the twelfth century, and they were dedicated to educating and taking care of the poor, as well as enforcing Christianity by military action. Their motto was

41

Helfen, Wehren, Heilen
Or
Help, Defend, Heal

The Knights survived the centuries and became a charitable institution. They were outlawed in Europe by Hitler in 1938, but regrouped in 1945, and are still active today although as a much smaller body. This monastery also survived through the centuries but by1945 was left a derelict ruin.

Jože Plečnik, who was 80 years old by then, was asked to transform it into something usable for the Ljubljana Festival in 1952. The church has survived pretty much intact, but the rest of the monastery was transformed into the Krizanke Summer Theatre. Have a good look around as you can still see some remnants from the original monastery, statues, archways and layers of decorative plaster (sgraffito).

The theatre itself is only open during the Ljubljana Summer Festival so you should check if there is something on which appeals: http://www.ljubljanafestival.si/en/

When you exit, turn right to reach the front of the church. If you look to the left of the door you will see a Roman tombstone built into the wall of the church. It was placed there by Plecnik who liked to bind the centuries together by reusing ancient relics.

Now continue past the pink church. The palace you see in front of you is the Auersperg Palace and houses the City Museum of Ljubljana.

Auersperg Palace

If you were intrigued by mention in the Potted History of the oldest wheel in the world, this is where you can see it. You can also see many Roman relics which were unearthed from Emona, the original Roman town which stood here.

Turn right into Gosposka ulica. The next street on your left is Križevniška ulica

Križevniška ulica

This is one of Ljubljana's prettiest and quirkiest streets. It's also one of the oldest streets in Ljubljana, and it was home to poets, actors and artists. The benches you see sprinkled down its length are decorated with political phrases or poems from across the world, and Ljubljana changes the words regularly. Stroll down to the riverside and turn right.

The Zois Pyramid and Mansion

The mansion on your right is the Zois Mansion, named after Baron Sigmund Zois, known as Baron Ziga Zois to the Slovenians. Zois was a great patron of the arts in Slovenia, and his Ljubljana home was a focal point of the city's intellectual circle. He was also a practical man so he built roads, a theatre, and a botanical garden. He died in Ljubljana, and his funeral was one of the biggest ever held in the city.

When you reach the bridge turn right to find the Plecnik's memorial to Zois. It's said that Plecnik tried to make his pyramid look as though it had grown out of the ground like the pyramids in Egypt. Actually it is looks more like the Pyramid symbol used by the freemasons - which fits because Zois was indeed a freemason.

Return to the riverside and the bridge

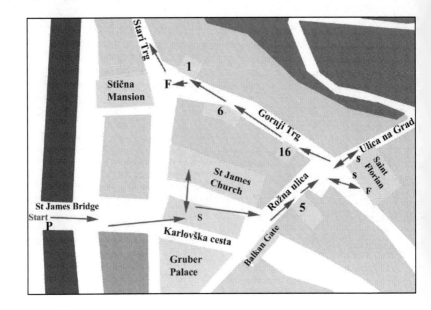

St James Bridge

On the right hand side pillar you can find the plaque which commemorates a watermill which stood here in the fifteenth century, but was destroyed in the 1515 Peasant Revolt. Cross the bridge.

Once on the other side walk straight ahead along Karlovška cesta toward the column and the church which you will see on the left hand side of the road.

Gruber Palace

Before you reach the column you will find the yellow Gruber Palace on your right – it is now the National Archive. It was originally built by architect and engineer Gabriel Gruber as a school of Hydraulics and Mechanics – he even added an observatory. He is best known for the Gruberjev kanal drainage channel which claimed back land from the marshes around Ljubljana. You can see his bust on the corner of the Palace as you approach it.

You can only see inside on an official tour arranged by the Tourist Office. But if the main door is open you could venture in to enquire and manage to peep at the lovely rococo stairway.

Cross the road to reach St James Church

St James Church

The column which stands outside is St Mary's column. It's another thank-you to God, this time giving thanks that the invading Turkish army had been defeated in battle in 1664.

The church was built by the Jesuits next to their monastery. The Jesuits always endeavored to educate the local population wherever they established their churches, and Ljubljana was no different. However they also interfered in politics and government and were generally disliked by the establishment. Over the centuries they were evicted from various European countries and finally abolished by the Pope in 1773. The college (which stood on Vodnik trg) took over the role of education when the Jesuits were expelled.

Plecnik redesigned this part of town and created the square the church looks onto. It's said he hated the church and planted the trees running along this side of the square to hide it. The church used to have two towers but they were badly damaged during the earthquake and had to be taken down. They were replaced by a single tower which was the highest in Ljubljana.

If the church is open go in – you might have to visit in the evening to catch it open. It has a famous main altar sculpted by Robba. To the left of the main altar is the more ornate octagonal Francis Xavier chapel which is adorned with a White Queen and Black King. Saint Francis founded the Jesuits and the statues represent the people of Europe and Africa met by Saint Francis on his journeys.

When you exit, turn left to return to Karlovška cesta. Continue along the street to reach the Balkan Gate which straddles the street and was part of the old town wall. Turn left at the gate to reach Rožna ulica. At number 5 on the right you will see a plaque mentioning Preseren. It marks the building in which he wrote his first sonnet of his "Wreath of Sonnets" which was dedicated to Julija.

Keep on Rožna ulica to reach a crossroads with Gornji trg. You are now in the old town.

Saint Florian

The parish church is on this crossroads and dedicated to St Florian. He was a Roman Commander in charge of a specialised group of soldiers whose task it was to fight fires. He became a saint when he refused to sacrifice to the Roman Gods and ironically was sentenced to be burned at the stake. As a soldier approached to light the pyre Florian declared

"If you do, I will climb to heaven on the flames."

The commander changed his mind and instead had him thrown into a river tied to a millstone. Saint Florian is the patron saint of firefighters.

When this part of town caught fire and burned to the ground in the seventeenth century, the locals decided to dedicate their new church to St Florian in the hope he would protect the rebuilt houses from further fires.

The current St Florian church was rebuilt by Plecnik. He replaced an old door at the front of the church with a fountain. Just next to it is a statue of St John of Nepomuk. St John was thrown into the river Vltava from the Charles Bridge in Prague by order of King Wenceslaus IV of Bohemia. Perhaps it was chosen since the two saints both ended up drowning.

Round the corner in Ulica na grad you can see a commemoration of Ljubljana's Roman heritage with a bust of an imaginary citizen of Emona – although he does look very sombre.

If the church is open pop in. You can find the portrait of Our Lady of Sorrow which is where the townspeople turned in times of disaster or calamity - September 15th is a holiday of Our Lady of Sorrow.

Face St John of Nepomuk and turn left to go down Gornji trg.

Gornji trg

Walk through a lovely old part of the town with the best preserved medieval houses. As you do, you can spot some markers:

At number 16 on your left is a plaque commemorating Valentin Metzinger, a French artist who worked most of his life in Ljubljana and lived in this building. His paintings are sprinkled around the churches of Ljubljana and if you visited the Ursuline church earlier you would have seen his work adorning the side chapels. If you venture in to the National Gallery of Slovenia during your visit you can see more of his work.

At number 6 on your right you can see two of the best preserved medieval houses – which always have three windows spaced across the width of the building on the top floor.

At number 4 is a plaque commemorating Baltazar Hacquet – a scientist who you probably have not heard of. He was a surgeon but also the first botanist to explore and investigate the Julian Alps which are part of the border between Slovenia and Italy.

Finally at number 1 on the right, look up to see an ancient depiction of Saint Christopher on the first floor – it dates from 1530.

Hercules Fountain

The road will have opened out now and you will see the Hercules Fountain. The statue is actually a modern replacement for the original 16th century statue which is now safely stashed away in the Town Hall. You will visit the Town Hall later. Hercules is shown clubbing a lion to death. The lion represents the ever-present threat of Turkish invasion. Hercules is facing east, the direction the Turks would arrive from.

Also find the plaque just next to the fountain which has some appropriate lines from Slovenian poet Janez Menart:

Day follows day, year follows year; while water merrily sprouts from the fountain. Passerby, remember: life is slipping away like water; so while there is time, catch it with your hands and drink it!

Stična Mansion

Behind Hercules is the grand Stična Mansion. It was actually built in the seventeenth century to house the abbots of the Cistercian Monastery in Stična, a nearby village. The monastery is the oldest in Slovenia, and it seems a bit odd that abbots didn't actually live in it. The mansion now houses the Academy of Music so you might here some music tinkling as you pass.

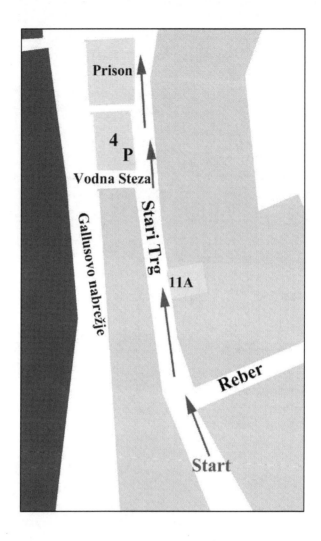

Face the Stična Mansion and turn right into Stari trg which is another narrow street of the old town.

Schweiger House

When you reach number 11a on the right you can spot the impressive doorway of the Schweiger House. It was commissioned by a court official called Schwieger who owned the house at the time.

At the top of the door is a titan holding his finger to his lips to suggest silence – that is because Schweiger means "one who keeps quiet".

The lady on the left of the doorway is Lili Novy, another of Slovenians much loved poets. She lived in the Schweiger House for a lengthy period.

Janez Valvasor

Pass Vodna steza on your left, and at number 4 you will find a plaque marking the birthplace of Janez Valvasor who was a prolific writer about the history of Slovenia in the seventeenth century. You won't have heard of him or his lengthy works, but you might have heard of another of his topics – he was the first to write about vampires.

Not Count Dracula of course, but Jure Grando who lived in a town called Krinja in what is now modern-day Croatia. Grando died in 1656 and the legend recorded by Valvasor tells us that he rose from the grave every night as a vampire. Finally the villagers dug his coffin up and found Grando's preserved body with a smile on his face. They sawed his head off, and as they did Grando screamed and finally died.

Just next door where the street is at its narrowest was an old prison - executions were carried out just outside. Look closely at the iron bars on the door at the front - you can see two blindfolded ladies holding the scales of justice, and Justica written between them.

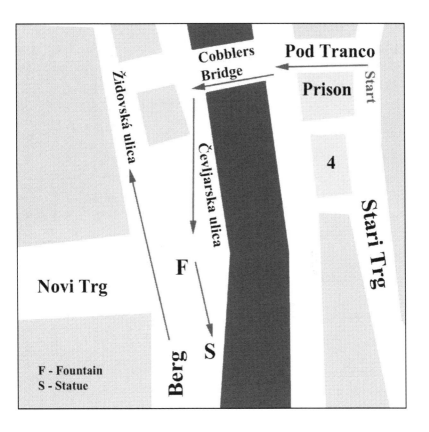

Take the next on the left, Pod Trančo which leads to Cankarjevo nabrežje and Cobblers Bridge.

Cobblers Bridge

The original wooden bridge which stood here is thought to be the oldest bridge in Ljubljana – and might originally have been a drawbridge from the thirteenth century. For some reason Ljubljana's shoemakers congregated on the bridge and around it, hence the name.

It was replaced by an iron version in the mid eighteenth century, and it lasted for 65 years before being moved when something more pleasing was wanted. This version is a Plecnik bridge, lined with six pairs of pillars to hold up the roof which Plecnik originally planned, but it never got completed. You might want to take photos of this pretty bridge.

Novi trg

Once on the other side of the river, turn left along Cankarjevo nabrežje. Just a few steps further on is Novi trg or New Square. You will see a large fountain, and behind it at the top of Novi trg you can see the back of the Library you visited earlier.

Continue along the riverfront to reach a large statue at the water's edge. This is Ljubljana's much respected Mayor Ivan Hribar which was erected in 2010 to celebrate the 100th anniversary of his term as mayor.

Jewish Quarter

Make your way back to the fountain. Take the street behind the building just ahead of you.

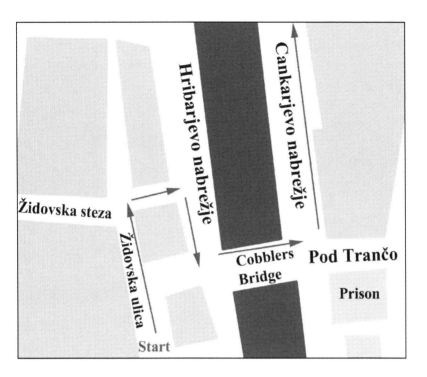

This will take you into Židovska ulica. Keep straight ahead passing a little café filled square to reach a crossroads with Židovska steza. You are now in the centre of what was the old Jewish quarter.

The Jewish people settled in this tiny area in the thirteenth century, and lived here for centuries in peace unlike many other parts of Europe. However in 1515 they were expelled by order of Holy Roman Emperor Maximilian I and Ljubljana's Jewish culture disappeared for centuries. They did return though in small numbers only to be devastated by the horrors of World War II. Today there is a small Jewish community, and they even opened a synagogue in 2003.

Turn right down Židovska steza to return to the river. Once at the riverside, turn right to reach Cobblers Bridge again and recross it to return to Cankarjevo nabrežje. Turn left and you will find that this side of the river is lined with lots of cafes and restaurants if refreshments are needed.

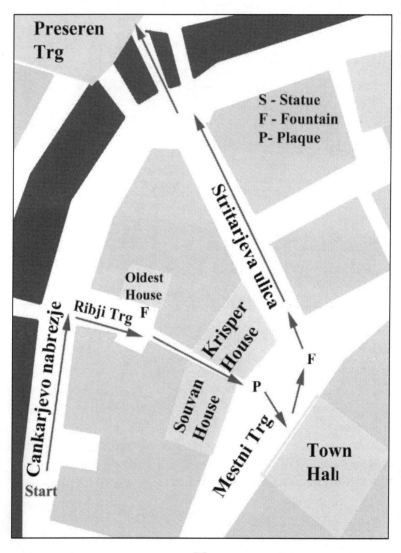

You will reach an unnamed little wooden bridge where you should turn right into a little square called Ribji trg

Ribji trg

This is Fish Square - in the sixteenth century there was a fish market and a river fishing pier here – all gone now. The little fountain in front of you has a Grecian woman standing on a pedestal which is decorated with three portrayals of the Greek water god Poseidon – very fitting for Fish Square.

Walk right up to the fountain and face the golden statue. The house on your left is the oldest house in town, built in 1528. It was the home of Primož Trubar who was a reformer and followed the teachings of Martin Luther. That resulted in his arrest being ordered by the church, so Trubar fled to Germany where he became the author of the first printed book in the Slovenian language. The house is now a café.

Leave by the pretty little lane behind the fountain – it's covered by arches, and at night it is lit up by Plecnik lamps. It will take you out to Mestni trg, or Town Square

Town hall

Right in front of you is the splendid Town Hall with its arches and balconies and pretty clock-tower.

Like many cities in Europe, Ljubljana has had its own dark periods of religious intolerance. In 1600 eight wagons full of protestant books were unloaded in front of the Town Hall and burned. There is a plaque marking the spot between the Town Hall and the archway just opposite.

In the 1920's there was a monument at the Town Hall entrance to King Peter I, the first Yugoslavian King. However Fascist Italy destroyed it when they annexed Ljubljana.

You can go inside and have a look around the ground floor. The first courtyard you reach has Robba's Narcissus Fountain tucked away in the corner, as well as several wall paintings depicting key moments in Ljubljana's history.

There is some lovely artwork on the arches around the courtyard
– spot the tower with the legendary dragon on top.

One of the archways lead into a second courtyard, and just above
it is a large 17th century map of Ljubljana.

The second courtyard is usually much quieter than the first, and it has an old well in the middle. There are often art displays in this courtyard.

Souvan House

As you leave the Town Hall, pause to look at the handsome mansion with its white pilasters which sits just opposite the Town Hall. That is the Souvan House and is one of the tallest buildings in the square. Running along the first floor is a set of sculptures representing trade, art and agriculture.

Robba Fountain

Just beside the Town Hall is the Robba Fountain which is Ljubljana's most famous fountain. As you might suspect, this is a replica and the original is in a museum

Robba was inspired by the Fountain of the Four Rivers in Rome, and this one is sometimes called the Fountain of Three Carniolan Rivers. The rivers are the Ljubljanica, Sava and Krka, and the steps apparently represent the Carniolan Mountains. The statues are made from Carrara marble, Michelangelo's absolute favourite stone. The other parts of the fountain are made from a local stone because the ship bringing the rest of the Italian marble sunk en route.

Krisper House

The building directly opposite the Town Hall and on the corner of Stritarjeva ulica is the Krisper House. This is where Julija Primic, the inspiration of the Slovene Romantic poet France Prešeren was born in 1816.

The composer Gustav Mahler also lived there in the late nineteenth century when he was a conductor at the Philharmonicorum in Kongresni trg which you saw earlier. Ljubljana decided to commemorate his stay by placing a bust on the house – it's on the ground floor opposite the Town Hall.

With the Robba Fountain behind you walk straight ahead down wide Stritarjeva ulica to the riverside. Cross the Triple Bridge to reach Preseren trg once more.

Walk 3 – Museums and Politics

This walk starts in Kongresni trg.

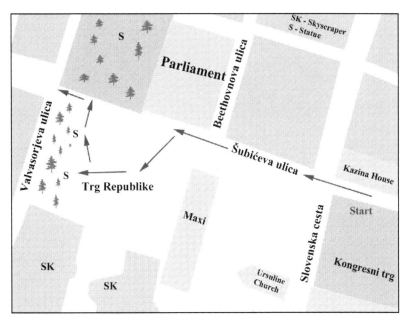

Face the Kazina House, and turn left to leave the square by Šubićeva ulica. Pass Beethovnova ulica on your right to reach the Parliament Building

Parliament Building

It's officially called The National Assembly Building. It actually opened in 1959 as The People's Assembly of the Republic of Slovenia since Slovenia was still part of Yugoslavia at that time. It became the Parliament Building in 1991 when Slovenia broke free and became an independent country.

It's actually a very modest building compared to the original Parliament Building planned by Plecnik. It's only extravagant feature is the sculpture surrounding the main doors, which in true communist style represents the ordinary man. Apart from that it could pass for an office block.

Opposite is Trg republike or Republic Square

Trg republike

This is a big bland square. Its designer dug up the Ursuline garden which belonged to the Ursuline Church you saw earlier. It was the largest garden in Ljubljana from the seventeenth century, and it was sacrificed to create this concrete square!

When the diggers moved in to create it, they discovered a wealth of Roman Ruins including walls over four meters high. If you look to the left side of the square you can see the Maxi market building. Part of the Roman wall was left in place so if you are really keen you could go down to the underground shopping arcade to see it. The diggers also found four large roman buildings and an altar to Jupiter, where the skyscrapers on the far side of the square now stand.

You will shortly see some very nice embassy buildings, but unfortunately the British embassy is not one of them. It is somewhere in one of those two ugly skyscrapers!

Today the square is only really decorated by two memorials on the right hand side. The very large one nearest to Parliament is The Monument to the Revolution, and the crowd scene further down the square commemorates politician Edvard Kardelj. He was a leader of the Communist party before World War II and of the Liberation Front of the Slovenian People.

Continue along Šubičeva ulica until you reach the end of the park on your right. As you do, you will see a statue of Janez Valvasor in the middle of the park. You might remember that name if you have done walk 2 – he was the author who first wrote about vampires.

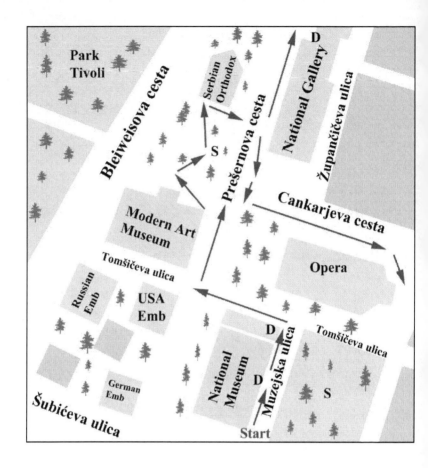

The next building on your right is the National Museum of Slovenia. Turn right alongside the park to reach the front door.

National Museum of Slovenia

This grand museum was built in 1883 and originally called the Rudolfinum after Crown Prince Rudolf. He committed suicide with his mistress at a hunting lodge in Austria, causing a huge scandal in European society.

Entrance is included in the Ljubljana card. Even if you don't have a Ljubljana card, it would be worth popping in just to see the Robba Fountain. Note, at the time or writing the Fountain is undergoing restoration.

The museum contains various artefacts which have been found in Slovenia stretching back to Neolithic times, and if you are in the mood you could spend a few hours perusing the exhibits. So if you decide to browse, climb the magnificent stairway draped with statues to explore. Probably the best exhibits are:

Oldest instrument in the world
Even if nothing else interests you, you might be intrigued to learn that the oldest musical instrument in the world was found in Slovenia. It's a 60,000 year old Neanderthal flute made from a leg bone - possibly of a cave bear.

Egyptian Mummy

How did an Egyptian mummy end up in Ljubljana? Well it was given by Anton Lavrin who was the Austrian consul in Egypt. It's quite spooky because the wooden coffin is inscribed with wording from the Egyptian Book of the Dead – and as any fan of The Mummy films knows, that is how you bring a Mummy back to life!

The coffin is also inscribed with the Mummy's name and profession – he was a priest in the temple of the God Amun in Karnak, Egypt.

Emona citizen
You will have seen a replica of this statue if you have already tackled Walk 2. This is the original, and it's quite unique - it's the only surviving Roman statue from a column, representing someone not in the ruling Roman family.

When you exit the museum turn left.

Roman tombstones

You will find the entrance to a glass extension to the museum which is where the museum has stashed its Roman tombstones. Even if you didn't go into the museum itself you could have a look around the tombstones as entrance is free.

When you exit turn left and then left again into Tomšičeva ulica. Walk straight ahead towards Prešernova cesta.

USA Embassy and Russian Embassy

As you approach Prešernova cesta you will see a pretty building across the street with the USA flag in the garden. Just behind the American Embassy is the Russian Embassy- but you would have to turn left along Tomšičeva ulica if you want a closer look. Let's hope they are good neighbours.

Turn right along Prešernova cesta

Museum of Modern Art

The very utilitarian looking building on your left is the Museum of Modern Art. However it is a bit more fun at the front as there are usually a couple of eccentric statues to have a look at.

The museum is well regarded but whether you would enjoy its content depends on your feelings towards modern art. It's included in the Ljubljana card.

Once past the museum you will see the grand National Gallery on your right and what looks like the entrance. However the public entrance is now further along Prešernova cesta. Before you get that far, approach the road running along the front of the museum. As you do glance to the left to see the entrance to the Tivoli Park – an enormous area of greenery which will take more time than you probably have to spare to explore. So cross the road instead to find the statue of Trubar amongst the trees and bushes on your left.

Trubar

If you have completed Walk 1, you might remember reading about Trubar who lived in Ljubljana's oldest house. He was a protestant reformer, but most famous as the author of the first book printed in Slovenian. He was also the founder of Protestantism in Slovenia and translated the bible into Slovenian. He is a revered national figure; they produced a television series based on his life and he has appeared on Slovenian banknotes.

Serbian Orthodox church

Behind Trubar is the Serbian Orthodox church with its ornate five domes – it was only opened in 2005. Inside is a kaleidoscope of colour, so if it's open do pop in to see it – it's worth it.

Now cross Prešernova cesta to the National Gallery entrance.

National Gallery

The museum doesn't contain any well-known works of art, but if you enjoy art it's worth a visit. It's included in the Ljubljana card.

The Gallery itself has been restored and is a work of art itself, with a gorgeous Grand Staircase, the Golden Hall and the Grand Hall.

So if you have time to wander around you will find lots to see – and you could hire a handy audio-guide at the desk. Another option is the guided tours which only last 45 minutes – but they are only run in July and August.

When you exit turn left to backtrack and take the first left into Cankarjeva cesta. You will soon see the lovely opera house on your right.

Opera House

Well it's mostly lovely. Unfortunately a grotesque modern black cube extension was added to it in 2011 and now looms over the original graceful pink building. However make your way around to the front and you can take a photograph without the cube.

When the Opera house first opened it was so popular that everyone who visited it wanted to let their friends know they had been there. So they sent postcards as proof – not unlike today's tourists sending photos of famous places by phone.

If you are interested in Opera or Ballet, check this link to see if there is anything interesting on during your visit.

http://www.opera.si/en/programme/what-s-on/

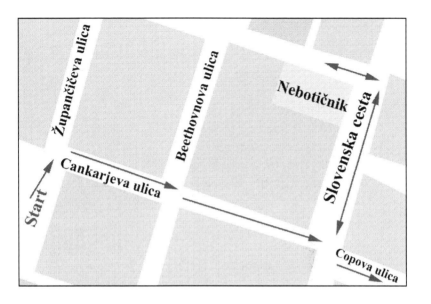

With the front of the opera house behind you turn diagonally left to rejoin Cankarjeva cesta. Turn right to go down Cankarjeva cesta. Cross over Beethovnova ulica and into a pedestrianised section of Cankarjeva cesta.

Once you reach Slovenska cesta, cross over the street and look left along Slovenska cesta to spot the modest skyscraper at the corner of the next junction. That is Nebotičnik.

Nebotičnik

It's only thirteen stories high but was the tallest building in Yugoslavia when it was built in 1933, and the ninth tallest in Europe. Given Ljubljana's earthquake history the builders applied strict Japanese anti-earthquake technology making it the most earthquake-proof building in Ljubljana

Its roof-top café was restored and reopened in 2010. If coffee or cocktails appeal you could do worse.

http://www.neboticnik.si/en/cafe-terrace.

If that little diversion does not appeal to you, continue the walk from Page 73 at Copova ulica.

Cocktail Diversion

To reach Neboticnik, turn left down Slovenska cesta then left again into Štefanova ulica. The entrance is at number 1. You have the choice of the elevator or a challenging spiral stairway to take you to the top.

When you are ready to move on, exit the building and turn right on Štefanova ulica, and immediately right again to return to Slovenska cesta. Walk back to the crossroads and turn left into Čopova ulica.

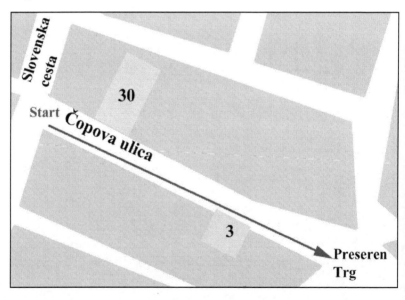

Copova ulica

Walk down Copova ulica. At number 30 on your left you will see a lovely art nouveau bank which has been converted into the Hostel Tresor. Even the bank's vaults are now bedrooms. It has some interesting statues guarding the doors.

Further down you will soon reach number 3 on the right where you can see a nice bronze art-nouveau sign – the only surviving art-nouveau sign in the city. It has lovely typical twining vines encircling the letters, and a little beehive at one corner which represents thrift. The beehive is fitting as this was the Ljubljana Municipal Savings Bank which was established in 1882. It was the first Slovenian bank and competed with the much larger German Kranjska Hranilnica bank. Apparently the interior is also art-nouveau but unfortunately it is not open to the public. Higher up you will see two figures representing Trade and Commerce. It's still a bank today.

Continue down Copova ulica to reach Preseren trg which is where this walk ends.

Walk 4 – Roman Ljubljana

This walk will take you a little further out of town to see what remains of Roman Ljubljana and into two ancient suburbs of Ljubljana.

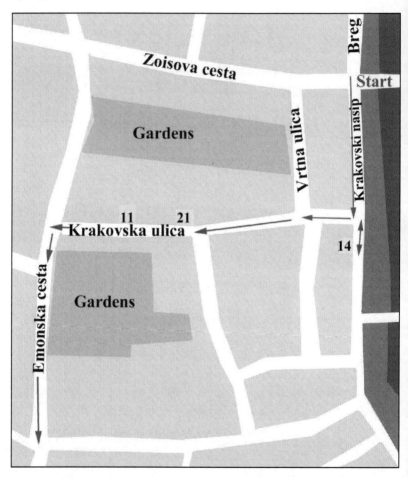

The walk starts at the St James Bridge on the opposite side of the river from the Castle. Face away from the bridge and turn left to walk down Krakovski nasip along the riverside.

Walk a few steps past Krakovska ulica on your right, and find the house at number 14.

Plague marker

Above the door you can see a little sleeping angel. It marks one of the last deaths from the plaque which struck Ljubljana 1599. The population of Ljubljana crashed from 20000 to just 6000 survivors in two years. You will see another shortly.

Backtrack a few steps and turn left into Krakovska ulica.

Krakovo

This was originally a little fishing village and the name Krakovo probably came for the Slovenian name for a marsh plant which grew here, "krak". This is a protected historical region full of little houses built in the traditional way.

These days Krakovo is full of market gardens. The various fruit and veg markets you see around Ljubljana are often filled with produce from the locals' gardens like the ones you will see here.

Krakovska ulica

Find number 21 and you will see another small carving, this time of an angel holding an hourglass. It's another plague death marker.

Now find number 11 on your right hand side. This is where Rihard Jakopič, Slovenia's greatest impressionist painter, was born. There is a plaque to mark the spot. You may have seen some of his paintings in the museums of Walk 3.

Jakopič's grandmother started the family sauerkraut business but it was his father who expanded their market. They did very well, selling their pickled cabbage as far away as South America. After the earthquake of 1895 the Jakopič family donated 200 huge barrels as temporary accommodation for the homeless!

Continue along Krakoska ulica to a T-juction and turn left down Emonska cesta - you will see lots of little allotments on your left all bursting with veg. There are fears though that their time is limited. It seems the younger generation is not as keen on gardening as their parents, and the allotments are not used as much as they used to be.

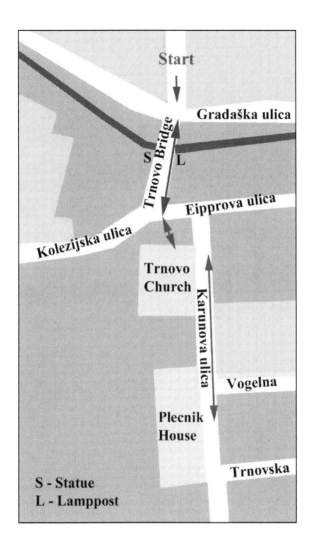

Ahead of you is the Trnovo Church and to reach it you will cross the Trnovo Bridge

Trnovo Bridge

It crosses Ljubljana's other little river, the Gradaščica, and is the boundary between Ljubljana's oldest suburbs Krakovo and Trnovo.

At this end of the bridge there is a tablet stating KRAKOVU and you will see another at the other end which says TRNOVU.

You might guess the bridge was designed by Plečnik when you spot the pyramids at each end! Plečnik was born in Trnovo and he designed and landscaped large parts of it.

Two rows of birch trees keep the cars separate from the people and make the bridge so pretty. In the middle you will see a statue of St John the Baptist – welcoming you over towards his church. Opposite the saint is a slim pyramid-shaped lamppost, dedicated to Zois who you read about on Walk 2.

Trnovo

Trnovo is not quite as old as Krakovo and its residents were traditionally boatmen. The name Trnovo is derived from the word Trn which means thorn, from the thorny bushes which were abundant here.

An old suburb of Ljubljana seems an unlikely place for rap music, but as you cross over into Trnovo you might be interested to know that Slovenia's biggest rap star came from Trnovo, Klemen Klemen.

Trnovo Church

You read about the unrequited love of France Preseren on Walk 1, and you will remember that it's believed he first saw Julija Primic near Preseren Trg. However it's also said that it was in 1883 in front of this church that he first laid eyes on her. Take your pick!

The church you see is not quite the same church as it was damaged in the 1895 earthquake, and when they repaired it they also redesigned it.

Face the front of the church and go down its left hand side. Just past the church you will find Plecnik's House which is now a museum.

Plecnik House

The museum is actually in two adjacent single storey houses. Plecnik's brother first bought just one of them. When Plecnik returned to Ljubljana he moved in with his brother, and they bought the house next door to expand into.

The museum showcases his work, both the plans which were used and perhaps more interestingly the ones which weren't – including the proposed new pyramid shaped Slovenia Parliament.

The museum has retained the house as it was when Plecnik lived there. However if you want to visit the house you have to book a place on a guided tour and places are limited

http://www.mgml.si/en/plecnik-house-503/

Now backtrack to the Trnovo Bridge and re-cross it.

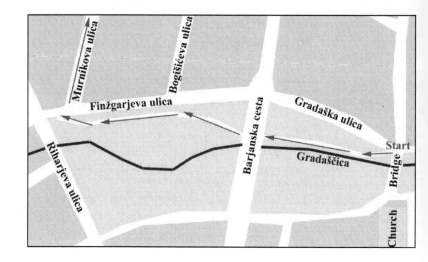

The Gradaščica

You will see a little path leading down to the riverside on your left. Go down and follow the path along the stream. Go under a bridge and continue along the riverside towards the next bridge. As you walk along the Gradaščica you can imagine the washerwomen who did their laundry in the stream and laid the garments out on the lawns and steps to dry.

Take the path back up to the main road just before the next bridge and you will find yourself on Finžgarjeva ulica. This little diversion avoids a very boring walk along a busy road.

Once on Finžgarjeva ulica stand with the river behind you and you will see busy Riharjeva ulica crossing the bridge on your left. Instead walk into Murnikova ulica which is just to the right of Riharjeva ulica. After a few minutes you will reach Mirje.

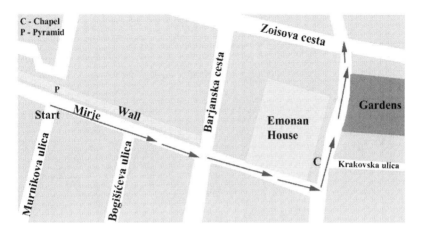

C - Chapel
P - Pyramid

Roman Wall

In front of you and stretching left and right is the Roman Wall of Emona.

The Romans built a stronghold here in the 1st century BC, and Emona itself was built in AD 14 by order of Emperor Tiberius. It was of course defended with sturdy Roman walls, and in front of you stretching left and right, are the remains of the Roman Wall of Emona.

Not surprisingly the wall was much bigger than the remains you see today. It's thought it was about 20 feet high, about 7 feet thick, and guarded by 26 towers. It also had a defensive moat running around three sides of the town – the fourth side was defended by the hill the castle sits on.

Romans loved straight lines and their cities and roads were laid out in strict linear fashion. So imagine this wall as one side of a large rectangle stretching up to Kongressi Trg where you saw the Roman Patrician on Walk 2.

Emona became a prosperous town, full of merchants and craftsmen. It was helped by the fact it lay on the Amber Road – an ancient trade route which merchants used to bring amber from the coastal cities of the North Sea to the Mediterranean. Amber was a precious commodity, sometimes called the gold of the North, and long ago it was even traded from the North Sea to faraway Egypt.

We are lucky to be able to see the wall these days. After World War I the city council decided to tear it down and sell off the land. Step up France Stelé who was head of the city's Monuments Office. He brought the plans to the notice of the public and raised such an outcry that the plans were changed to a restoration.

Directly opposite you will find a rather out-of-place pyramid built into the wall. Yes the restoration project was given to Plecnik and it seems he couldn't resist improving the original Roman construction.

Cross over and turn right to walk down Mirje with the wall on your left. As you do have a look at the wall closely and you will see a small irregular line of white stones running along it. They were placed there by Plecnik to mark the boundary between the original wall and his reconstruction.

Cross Barjanska cesta and continue down Mirje. At number 4
you will find the Emonan House

Emonan House

This is a small archeological park letting you see what's left of
the home of a Roman family from the 4th century. The experts have
decided that the family was wealthy because the diggers have
unearthed a floor decorated with coloured mosaics, which only the
very well-off could possibly afford. They also had Roman central
heating and even sewers which were very advanced for the time.

There is a charge to get in and to be honest if you have visited
one Roman ruin before you won't see much that will surprise you,
but if you are a fan of Roman ruins you will want to visit.

At the end of Mirje turn left into Emonska Cesta to return to
Krakovo. You will pass a little chapel on your left.

Krakovska Kapela

This tiny little chapel used to contain an ancient Slovenian
carving of Mary with the baby Jesus. It was made in the 13th
century and was part of the old Krizanke church which you read
about on Walk 2. In the eighteenth century they decided to rebuild
that church so the carving was moved to this chapel. The original is
now safely in the Ljubljana National Gallery but at least a replica
has been placed in the chapel.

Continue along Emonska Cesta and you will soon see more
market gardens on your right. At the end of the street you will reach
Zoisova cesta where this walk ends.

You can turn right to make your way back to the riverside, or
perhaps walk straight ahead to head towards to Kongresni trg.

Did you enjoy these walks?

I do hope you found these walks both fun and interesting, and I would love feedback. If you have any comments, either good or bad, please review this book.

You could also drop me a line on my amazon web page.

BRAINS ARE THE NEW TITS

Ten Rules for Following Your Dreams by

Using Your Brain

By Hanna Kinsella

Chapters

Introduction

Introduction

When I was lucky enough to be offered the chance to join the cast of *Real Housewives of Cheshire*, I was worried I wouldn't quite fit in.

After all, here was a glamorous group of feisty housewives and I'm the owner of a dental practice – as far from a housewife as you can possibly get! I worked at least 40 hours a week and every dress in my wardrobe I've bought myself. One of my first sentences on the show was: *'Own your success and earn your own dress – it will feel so much better!'*

So how was this going to go down with the others?

Thankfully straight away I clicked with Seema, owner of the Forever Unique brand, and Dawn, a footballer's wife who's set up her own businesses. But just as quickly the other ladies didn't know what to make of me.

For the first time in my life, I heard critical remarks about the fact I'd graduated from university. One housewife even made a pretend snoring sound as she rolled her eyes and said: *'Five years of medical school – zzzzzz.'* (It was eight years and it was dental school, but never mind!)

Not being a cocky show-off, I couldn't understand this reaction. I'm no better than anyone else; I've just chosen a different path. I'm not one to judge others, as we all make our own life choices.

But then something happened. After my first few appearances on the show, my Instagram following shot up from 700 to over 48,000 within weeks and I started to get flurries of messages from viewers.

'*Dan_moore1990 You're such an inspiration @hannamiraftab <3*'

'*Roxie_fitness Amen!!! I think you are totally the right person to be on RHOC because you truly portray how hard work and determination will propel you in life and not mean you have to depend on anyone other than yourself; that there is more to life than just what's on the exterior!!! #brainsbeforebeauty #beingaboss*'

'*Carly_x_alty I don't usually comment on IG posts but what you've said about taking opportunities... thank you! That's just what I needed to hear today xx*'

'*Heathertaylormann Loved you on this series, a great role model for little girls watching x*'

'*Notridge2018 I have loved watching you from the beginning to end a refreshing change from the usual housewife. Question is can you put yourself through another season with certain housewives?!'*

'***Carolineturner2018*** *Hi Hanna, you are a great inspiration to educated ladies and bring a different slant to the Real Housewives franchise. Keep going, albeit I love love love Dawn, Tanya, Seema and the rest.'*

To my amazement, I had mums, teenage girls and young lads all telling me I was like a breath of fresh air on reality TV. They were thanking me for talking about the importance of education and hard graft in life. I had messages from young girls to say they wanted to be like me and mums who said I was a good role model for their daughters.

In all honesty, I was absolutely gobsmacked, but also deeply touched. Then shortly afterwards I posted a quote I love on Instagram:

Brains are the new tits.

It made me laugh, but it also rings true. We've all seen young women aspire to being footballers' wives or girlfriends or long to be beautiful above anything else. We've also all heard how women are judged for wanting to be glamorous in a working environment or absorbed the message society gives us girls which says:

You can be clever or beautiful, but not both.

But I say otherwise. I LOVE fashion, having my hair done, bold makeup and dressing up. I love designer clothes and strutting about in a good pair of heels and taking the odd glammed-up selfie. And… I ALSO love my job, earning and spending my own money and being independent. I'm proud to care about what I look like and am passionate about my work.

I love the glam but I'm taken seriously as a successful cosmetic dentist and entrepreneur. And this is what I want to tell every woman out there, young or old: **Clever and beautiful? Yes, you *can* be both.**

Living in today's fast-moving world is not an easy task and at times it can be quite intimidating and off-putting, especially if you lack confidence and self-esteem. But by recognising your strengths, believing in yourself and following your dream you CAN draw your own path to success and happiness. And that's despite what's going on around you.

While there's a place for nice tits (fake or otherwise!), there is an even bigger place in our lives for our brains. We are all blessed with huge potential and our minds, alongside our dreams, can help us to reach those places. I want every reader of this book to feel inspired, because what happened to me can definitely happen to you too.

So that's what made me put pen to paper. The amazing *Real Housewives* fans have told me they want to hear how I made it, so here are a few rules I learned that helped along the way. And you don't need to rely on your tits to do it.

Love, Hanna x

Rule 1: Be a daydream believer

So rule number one is… there are no rules! Ha, well yes and no. However, because we're all individuals, we'll find different things that work for us. That's why in this book I have included other people's journeys of how they succeeded too.

My 'rules' are ideas of what I have learned along the way, but take whatever resonates with you personally. Saying that, if we want to live a life we love then there's one thing we could ALL do more of, and it starts with one very simple thing…

Daydreaming!

Yes, you did read that right. Daydreaming is where it all began for me and I believe it's where it could all begin for you too.

As a little girl, I grew up in a disciplined household with professional Iranian parents. I was the only 'off-white' girl in my class and didn't fit in. I had a monobrow and a funny surname and I wasn't very clever. But I didn't fit in at home either, because I wanted to join in Western culture, like drinking and partying, so my mum and dad worried about me. My life was happy and my parents were always supportive, but… I could not wait to grow up.

So one thing that kept me going was daydreaming. And it turned out I was a natural at it too. From about the age of nine, I dreamed of growing up to be a pretty woman. I dreamed of having a handsome husband (hello, Martin Kinsella!). I dreamed of a lovely car and home, and a life filled with friends and fun. I didn't know what I wanted to do at the time (being a dentist wasn't on my radar yet), but I knew what sort of person I wanted to be: fun, successful, happy, glamorous and living life to the full.

My favourite place to daydream was in the back of the car on long, boring journeys. We had no iPads and iPhones in those days, and looking back that was a good thing.

We all need space and time to allow daydreams to flourish. It's simple and it's free and you can start doing it today. Even right now. You don't have to be sitting at home staring at a wall to do it either. You could be going for a walk with the dog, or on your commute, or having some time to yourself with a cup of coffee in the afternoon. Wherever it is, allow yourself the time and space every day to think of where you are and *where you want to be*.

Don't be fooled that daydreaming is a waste of time either. Do you remember being told at school 'Stop dilly daydreaming!' when you gazed out the window? I certainly do. But there's a point to it, and science even backs this up.

Research by Dr Fiona Kerr, a cognitive neuroscientist at Adelaide University, has shown we can get a boost from having a little 'mini break in our heads' and it even helps us sort out complex things in our minds. It allows our brains, especially the subconscious part, the space and time to think about what we really want.

Before you begin, ask yourself: *'What do I really, really want?'* and allow your brain to go on a little journey for you.

It could be a nicer house, a holiday, a hobby you've secretly wanted to take up for ages, a new job you think you'd be good at, more friends, taking up something creative. It could be having kids, spending more time with your kids, or getting a dog or a cat or even a chameleon! It could be literally *anything.*

As I grew up, my daydreaming became more than just an outlet to imagine a life as an adult. Without really realising it, I'd started to powerfully visualise where I wanted to be and WHO I wanted to be in life, which is the basis of the Law of Attraction (more about this later).

Most importantly my daydreams taught me I deserved it too. If you believe in your daydreams, you're far more likely to achieve them. If you don't think you deserve anything better than what you already have, it will almost certainly go past you.

The older I became, the more the vision of a strong woman came into my head. I wanted to be independent and not rely on a man for money or to drive me everywhere. The women in my family were strong, but they needed their husbands to help them with ordinary tasks like filling the car with petrol or driving on the motorway.

But in my daydreams I was always the one in the driving seat!

Dare to dream

When you think about it, every single thing that man or woman has invented or succeeded at began with a single daydream. The person who discovered fire might have been daydreaming while playing with sticks, the person who invented the wheel daydreamed about a different way of moving… the list is endless.

Asking ourselves questions like *'Wouldn't it be amazing if…'* or *'What I'd really like is…'* or *'I can just imagine myself doing…'* can trigger all kinds of incredible chains of events. And yes, events we'd only ever dared dream about previously!

But daring to dream is just the beginning. I can tell you now: you deserve to have your dreams come true as much as the next person.

As part of this book I've spoken to many women who have shared their stories with me about how they succeeded in life. Marketing executive and mum Halima Khatun ('Halima' even means 'dreamer', how amazing is that?) told me how daydreaming helped her build a business.

Halima said, *'When I was little I was always imagining what my grown-up life would be like, but the older I got, the more "glass half-empty" I became. I used to say, "Better not be too hopeful or I'll jinx it." But once I came out of my comfort zone and set up my business, I decided to turn everything on its head.'*

Halima started to read self-help books like *The Miracle Morning* by Hal Elrod and she found a business coach to help her. During sessions the coach asked her to visualise what she wanted out of life and verbally describe it.

'I even had to describe where I was and what I was wearing,' Halima said. *'I wanted to work for myself in a successful business and start a family, so in my visualisation I even saw myself holding a baby girl!'*

Phew, this all sounds ambitious, doesn't it? But the fact is, Halima didn't stop her dreams, she ran with them. She let them flourish and let herself be guided by them. The belief it would happen gave her confidence to go for it, and gradually she set about building her PR business.

As things progressed with her business, Halima was lucky enough to fall pregnant in 2016 with – you guessed it – a baby girl! Halima, who now runs PR company HK Communications, didn't stop there. Her blog, called *halimabobs.com*, which started out as a hobby, featuring articles about everything from parenting to beauty treatments, has turned into a successful website which is widely read. She's also written pieces for *The Huffington Post* and been featured in national newspapers.

Anything can come true

Why limit yourself when the truth is, *anything* is possible? The power of daydreaming is so strong, you can even think up something you have no experience of and make it come true.

Take Yee Kwan's story. She set up her own ice cream business in 2009 with NO experience in food manufacturing. She simply loved ice cream!

She told me: *'I've always tried to live with a positive mental attitude and I read* The Secret, *which taught me to visualise using the Law of Attraction. I daydreamed about one day setting up a business with a food I loved, winning contracts with my dream customers, seeing my ice cream on menus, celebrating with my team, even going global. Crazy dreams some might say! But bit by bit this helped me define what it was I wanted.'*

Like Yee, I am also a big fan of the book *The Secret.* The book was a bestseller when it was published back in 2006 and it's based on a belief in the Law of Attraction, which says a person's thoughts (and daydreams!) can change their life directly. It's a step beyond daydreaming, as you write down what you wish to attract into your life and carve out time during the day to make positive steps towards it.

Yee started from scratch. She did her research about ice cream companies, went to manufacturing open days and then learned how to make her own ice cream! She then worked in her kitchen to develop recipes and tested them on customers at a local farmers' market. She sought financial help from local government grants to set up her little business. Ten years later, Yee Kwan Ice Cream is exporting to China and she's just signed a deal worth over

£2m. Of course it took a lot of hard work and focus, but it all began with one single dream.

Keeping your mind open

It wasn't until I reached my teenage years that I realised I'd need to focus on a career to make my dreams come true. But I didn't know what I wanted to be, so I set out to try lots of different work experiences. I wanted to do something creative. Something fun. But also pay for a decent lifestyle. So I worked in a lawyer's and an architect's office, with journalists and in a hospital, before I finally found a placement at a dental surgery.

Studying dentistry was definitely not on my top five or even ten list of things I daydreamed about. As someone who hated maths and sciences, it seemed like madness. But the fact is, the more you widen your net in life, the more experiences you have and the more opportunities come flooding in. Being open to anything is the best attitude, because how do you know if you'll like something unless you try it?

I was also lucky enough to come across an inspirational dentist on this placement. Perhaps my path might have been different if the dentist had been a misery guts who didn't make time to talk to me – I don't know. I could call it luck, but I also believe you create your own luck. If you cast your net wide enough, you'll eventually come across something that grabs you or someone who wants to help.

'What sort of career are you interested in, Hanna?' he asked me, in between seeing patients.

'Not sure,' I sighed. *'Something artistic hopefully. So I'm not sure dentistry will be for me.'*

'Aha,' he smiled. *'But dentistry is in fact very creative, because you are putting together a person's smile. And what can be more artistic than that?'*

His words made something click, and when the next patient came in for a check-up I was riveted by what the dentist was doing and saying. As I left the surgery that evening, I started daydreaming about doing the job myself. It paid good money and was a professional career. The more I dreamed, the more excited I became.

<u>Top tips for daydreaming</u>

1. **Put down your phone!** I'm serious. Technology is brilliant, but evidence suggests our phones and iPads etc. are filling the gaps of the day where we

could be doing important things like…
daydreaming! Set aside some time every day, even
if you start with just 15 minutes, to switch off and
zone out. Allow your mind to wander. Set a timer if
you need to. But just relax and enjoy it. See where
your dreams take you!

2. **Ask yourself some big and silly questions.** Ask
yourself what your biggest dream is. Go crazy and
think up scenarios you'd never even imagine you'd
imagine. Maybe if you're looking for a new flat you
might decide you want to live on a houseboat.
Maybe if you think you'd like a new boyfriend you
might really want a dog instead. Maybe you're
stuck in a rut with your friendship group and will
imagine having a fun, positive group of new mates
in your life. Whatever it is, NOTHING is off limits.
You could dream about feeling happier, freer,
healthier or fitter. It's okay to want more, even if
you're content with what you have too.

3. **Don't be afraid.** It might feel a bit weird at first.
But even science says daydreaming is not a waste of
time. It's good for us, and our brains. View it as a
workout for your mind and imagination.

4. **Trust.** You probably won't reap the rewards of daydreaming straight away, but that's okay. Trust that it will work, even in six months or a year's time. Once you start daydreaming and trusting in your thoughts, it will come more naturally to you and perhaps change the direction you want in life.

Rule 2: Choose your lane – and stick to it

So, you've daydreamed about a life you've always wanted. You believe in it. You hope it will come true. What next? Well, I believe you need to decide what path you want to follow and stick to it – at least for long enough to know if it will work or not.

This isn't always the easy bit. It takes some guts to even know for sure what you want. But making the effort to 'decide' on a path is one step towards getting it.

For me, I'd decided I wanted to go to university and study dentistry. But I was 14 and not very academic and my nickname at school was Hanna Mustafa. I was more interested in sneaking out of my bedroom to go drinking with my friends in a park than studying. So how was my dream going to happen?

First of all I told people. I told my parents, my friends, my teachers, anyone who would listen: *'I want to be a dentist.'*

Some of my mates laughed openly, others shrugged, while my best mates said it was a great idea and my poor parents (who at this point probably wondered what the hell I'd end up doing!) were thrilled to bits.

It was only the first step on my journey, but it was a major one. By sharing my intention in life, I was making myself more accountable. Even if I didn't know this at the time!

If we keep our heart's desires secret then we're less likely to follow them through. If you only 'secretly' want to do something, you might not feel as motivated to find out how to do it. Your inner voice might end up putting you off on a bad day. How many of us have thought *'Oooh, I've always wanted to do that'* but really we never properly explored the idea? It might be because we have pigeonholed ourselves as not being 'good enough', or we might think other people will laugh or our own inner critic might pipe up and destroy our ideas.

But if you tell people then at least you might find someone out there to encourage and support you. Because along the way that's what everyone needs at times. You might find that saying it aloud makes it more real too. So you're more likely to succeed and not give up before the journey has begun.

First steps: Program your subconscious

'A journey of a thousand miles must begin with a single step.' – Lao Tzu

There really is no better time to begin than now. Today. This second. Come on, what's stopping you?

After my first step of openly saying to someone 'I want to be a dentist!' I soon discovered that not everyone's reaction was supportive or positive. For example, when I told my careers advisor, I didn't quite get the reaction I was expecting from her.

'Well, Hanna,' she said, pointing to my flicked-style eyeliner, 'you'll have to get that makeup off your face for a start.'

At the time, I loved wearing outlandish makeup, carefully applied before the start of the school day, but instantly this teacher's response crushed me. She made me feel small, stupid and bad for wanting to wear makeup and for having an ambition to study dentistry. I walked away from Mrs McLellan's office with my head lowered, feeling belittled. Doubts clamoured in my mind:

Am I stupid for having such a dream?

Do I have what it takes to study such an academic subject?

Will my eye makeup put off future employers?

Was Miss right… do dentists not wear nice makeup?

I was absolutely filled with self-doubt just from this one comment made by someone in authority (when I look back now I think, frankly, this teacher was abusing that authority!).

For most of us, it doesn't take much to knock our confidence. Especially if we're trying something new or admitting what our dreams are. It doesn't take much for the nagging little voice inside to get louder and louder, until it's all we can hear.

You're not good enough.

Who do you think you are?

You can't do that…

You're not clever enough / strong enough / academic enough / [insert your own self-professed weakness here!].

But let's get one thing straight: ALL human beings have this persistent doubtful inner voice. It's human nature. So we have to challenge this and retrain our subconscious to recognise the voice and either ignore it or drown it out with a positive one.

What you put out there will come back!

The Law of Attraction teaches us that whatever we put 'out there' we will find in return. If you wake up moaning and groaning about your lot in life, you're more likely to have it reflected back at you. Think about it. If you begin your day in a bad mood, you focus on all the crappy things that annoy you and then you notice more of them.

Put simply, the Law of Attraction is the belief that 'all thoughts turn into actions', and many believe it's one of life's biggest mysteries. Even if you don't believe in a spiritual side of life, there can be little doubt that how we think and behave is bound to impact on our lives.

It's the same with people. If you look for the good in someone, you'll find it. If you look for something to criticise someone about, you'll also find it.

Taking back control of our self-talk is one of the biggest confidence-boosting things we can do for ourselves. It's a major stepping stone in helping the Law of Attraction to work.

For International Women's Day recently I was invited back to my old school in Bolton to do a talk about careers for Years 9 to 11. I told them funny stories about my work experiences and how I knew from early on what I wanted to be. One girl came up to me afterwards and said, *'I really liked what you said, Hanna, but I'm just not confident or good at speaking up like you. My friends all agree I am shy; it's not just me saying that either.'*

At this point I took her aside. *'Listen to me,'* I said gently. *'You have to stop telling yourself you are no good. I'm telling you now, you ARE good! You are at a good school, you have a great group of friends, and you can be whatever you want to be in this world, but you have to promise me you're going to start believing in it…'*

'Yes, maybe you're right,' she smiled.

As our conversation went on, I could see in the space of ten minutes this girl growing in stature and confidence. She smiled more, she looked more relaxed and she nodded as we chatted. Simply by learning there was another way of being – i.e. confident – she was already feeling better about herself. And that's what it's all about. If you can tell yourself you can do it then you're halfway there, even if it means 'faking it until you make it', but more on that later.

After my own career teacher dismissed my teenage dreams, I went home that night and looked in the mirror as I wiped off my eye makeup. I don't know where it came from, but I decided I wasn't going to allow some disbelieving teacher to stop me. Just like I didn't let my parents stop me having fun, I wasn't going to let this teacher pour cold water over my career idea before it'd even started.

Somehow I knew I had to do both. I had to be myself. Even if that meant studying for a serious profession whilst wearing all the makeup I wanted to, and enjoying myself along the way. But I needed to choose a lane so I could give it a good go. And it was then, thankfully, that my positive rebellious streak took over.

Be a positive rebel

Our society, education system, sometimes even our own families like to put us in boxes. We might be called the quiet one, the clever one, the funny one or the noisy one.

And these labels stick with us from an early age. If our parents tell us we're shy, we're more likely to be. If we fail our GCSEs, we might think an academic life isn't for us. If we're girls who love wearing dresses and high heels, we might think certain jobs are not for us.

But let me tell you, all this is bollocks! Sometimes we need to rebel against these labels to become who we really want to be. Instead of rebelling against a system so that we lose (like taking drugs or drinking or bunking off school etc.), we can rebel so that we win and end up with the lives we *really* want to live.

Let me tell you about Keira Walcott, a 22-year-old single mum who set up her own cosmetic brand called Kandor Cosmetics. Straight away you might think, *'Wow, she must have had some help there!'* But let me also tell you, Keira used to be so shy she couldn't look anyone in the eye and she was bullied for having a debilitating skin condition called vitiligo, where white patches develop on the skin. Then let me tell you that she left school with no GCSEs and became a single mother aged 16!

But instead of feeling sorry for herself and thinking about what she didn't have, Keira found her inner positive rebel and asked herself: *'Okay, I'm in this really hard situation with what appears to be no way out… but what is it I CAN do?'* By encouraging her rebellious side, Keira refused to be pigeon-holed as the poor, single, trapped mum and looked for other ways out. Here's her story, in her own words.

'I had a normal life until I went to secondary school and developed acne and vitiligo. Any makeup I used tended to make my skin worse, so I began to experiment with cover-ups using only natural ingredients. Then one day one of my

classmates left a note on my computer screen which said: "Learn how to do your makeup – you look disgusting."

I was so upset and wanted to run home and hide. Somehow, though, it made me more determined to try and find a better way of covering up too. I started experimenting with different products and doing as much research as I could. Inside lessons I never bothered to listen but makeup was the one thing I was passionate about.

I left school when I was 15 and by 16 found myself pregnant. By then I had little family support, so I ended up living in a hostel, alone with the baby.

This was the worst of times. Society tells us if you're a teenage single mum you're a no-hoper and achieving anything felt like a pipe dream. I hated living at the hostel, where everyone smoked weed and was happy to sit and do nothing all day. I needed to find another way.'

Keira refused to accept the label of being helpless and explored every avenue to find a way out. First of all she saved what little money she had, and then she asked a supportive family member to help with babysitting. Then came the next big step. Keira told me:

'I decided to look for ways I COULD do what I wanted to do. Following all my years of experimenting with cover-

27

ups, I daydreamed of starting my own makeup company. So I applied to The Prince's Trust, who work with vulnerable young people to teach them how to run a business. I ignored the voice in my head saying I stood no chance and filled in the application form anyway. I knew I had to try something. Then to my amazement I was offered a place on a business start-up course, which I loved. Next I applied to the Trust for a business loan to set up my company making cosmetic cover-ups for problem skin. I called it Kandor Cosmetics and started to sell it online a year later. Every time I did a tutorial on YouTube, I saw sales zoom upwards. By 2018 I was making a profit, and my next step is to market the product in shops. It's now my main income and how I support my family. This one little idea has gone way beyond my wildest dreams.'

Keira's story goes to prove that even when ALL the odds are stacked against you, when it seems truly hopeless, it's still possible to find your positive inner rebel and a way out.

Sacrifice is *not* a bad word

When reading other people's stories it's easy to feel overwhelmed about where to start on your own journey.

But everyone, whoever they are, begins with tiny first steps. It could mean googling the subject you're interested in, whatever that is, or ringing a college to ask about a course, or emailing someone who's already doing that job for advice.

In one single day you can make moves in the right direction. Even if it feels uncomfortable at first, it will get easier with each step. Then once you've decided which lane to 'stick to' it's good to be prepared to confront what's next. And that's a willingness to *sacrifice.*

Sacrifice sounds like a bad word. It conjures up the idea of denying yourself or being miserable. But it's necessary to accept that you will need to sacrifice some things to achieve whatever your end goal is.

Anything worthwhile WILL take time and your energy. It will mean you have to decide whether to focus on the fun elements of life or the stuff that takes hard work and dedication. Nobody is going to knock on your front door and give you your heart's desire (well, unless you've ordered a pizza, that is!).

Accepting the need to sacrifice is a good thing, because it hardens you up a bit for when you'll inevitably face those tough times.

I'm not a naturally bright person. I'm not academic. But I'd decided to be a dentist. So I had to suck up the sacrifice and quickly!

First of all I had to decide I needed to study and study hard. Dad helped me with my worst subject, maths, so I could pass my GCSE. I also had to suck up doing science A levels. I hated science, but now I had a goal in mind, it seemed less bad. I also had to sacrifice weekends out. I still partied, but was selective about when, so I didn't burn the candle too much at both ends. I needed reserves of energy left to study.

When times were hard and I felt at a low ebb, I just closed my eyes and thought about how brilliant it would be to have a good profession behind me. How proud I'd be to have gained a place at university to study dentistry. It was my goal and I just had to cling on to it.

Eventually I scraped by with my grades and managed to get an interview at Liverpool University. It was a face-to-face chat with a tutor, and I honestly think it was my enthusiasm and passion for the subject that impressed them! Sometimes a positive attitude and passion for a subject can mean more than qualifications.

That tutor who offered me the place must have spotted my willingness to sacrifice to get where I wanted to go.

If it's not hurting, it's not working

I don't like pain any more than the next person. But... if you want to get ahead, you have to be prepared to work hard for it. It's like going to the gym. We know it will make our muscles ache and be tiring, but if we want to tone up, that's the price we pay. It's the same with dieting. If you want to lose weight, you've got to be prepared to sacrifice eating whatever you want all day long. Just like we all know chocolate is fine in moderation but if we eat it all the time we'll feel sluggish and put on weight, so it's about balance. We need to learn to recognise when it's time for fun and when it's time to put the work in.

I'm a party girl. I love to go out. But I KNEW I'd have to rein it in to get what I wanted: qualifications to win a place to study dentistry. This meant missing out on holidays with my girlfriends to Ibiza and late boozy nights, and spending my money on books rather than clothes. My studies took priority, but I knew it wasn't forever and it would be worth it in the end.

The day the news came in that I'd won a place at university, I was actually jumping for joy. All the little sacrifices had been worthwhile, and even though I knew big hurdles were ahead, I was going to enjoy each little victory as it happened.

I started my university placement in 2006. On the day I arrived, I felt a stab of envy when I saw students get off the bus at St John Moore's university, a powerhouse for the creative subjects. They were all wearing fashionable clothing, piercings and tattoos, and I knew I'd fit into that arty crowd more. But this was the next part of the sacrifice I was making, because I also knew I really, *really* wanted to be a dentist. So I squared my shoulders, held my head high and joined all the science boffs wearing white trainers and baggy jeans on my new course.

You can have fun along the way, but EVERYTHING worthwhile takes time and effort. There might be such a thing as a free lunch (if someone else offers!), but when it comes to hard graft it's always tiring, a bit boring at times, or just plain frustrating. But anything worthwhile in the long run is never easy.

Rule 3: Find your inner resilience – we *all* have it

So you have chosen your lane, made a few sacrifices and made decisions about where you want to go. But what will happen along the way? Well, several things:

1. You will lose patience.
2. You might decide it's easier to give up.
3. You'll face unexpected challenges.

But I'm not here to make you want to give up! I'm helping you to accept what will happen along the way, so you can arm yourself with inner resilience. We set ourselves up to succeed rather than fail by finding the strengths we all have inside. Resilience is about preparing ourselves for when the going gets tough. Because it will do at times, and if we are prepared for it, we're far less likely to give up.

Before I left for university, I made a few decisions in my own mind about what sort of person I wanted to be when I went out into the world. I thought of different characteristics and explored these ideas. Luckily for me, I have good parents who support me in what I want to do, which helped me develop my own set of values.

Not everyone is so lucky. If your family are not supportive, then look for mentors elsewhere. You could find them at school in good teachers, at college, or even in extended family members or friends' parents. But more than anything, I believe you need to find the mentor inside of YOU!

What do I mean by this? Well, there's nobody who can cheerlead better than you can. It's easy to blame others for things not going well. Your teachers might be crap, your parents might have their own agenda when it comes to supporting a certain path (and let's face it, every parent who is supportive is wonderful, but also deep down they have their own 'stuff' going on – they might be pushing their own dreams onto you etc.) and good career advisors at school are often few and far between.

But if we look inside ourselves at the times we need it and learn to develop our own inner resilicnce and self-belief, then NOBODY can take it away from us.

I also looked elsewhere for role models and then decided who I wanted to be according to what I saw in other people.

Like Angelina Jolie. Not only is she the mum of six kids and a successful ambassador for the UN where her charity work spans the globe, but she's also an Oscar- and Emmy-award-winning actress! What I admire about her is her guts.

She doesn't seem to care what other people think and creates her own rules. She definitely embraces her inner rebel and helps others in the process. I also love her commitment to family, something I too as a new mum feel is important. All in all, her kick-ass attitude and her glam image make her a woman to look up to.

I also admire the Queen. She is the face of resilience. Despite all the ups and downs her family has been through she still shows up, puts on a brave face and does her duty for our nation. There is a lot to be said for that attitude in life. Over the years she has seen scandals happen around her, has put up with visits from world leaders and despite her old age has attended events all over the world for over half a century. But she's never faltered. She never shows lack of courage or gives up. She is a steady, solid figurehead who symbolises stoicism. Even if you're not a Royalist, she is someone to admire.

I also adore my mother. She has worked really hard in her job as a physiologist and a lecturer as well as bringing up me and my brother, but she's always kept a sense of humour and I enjoy her company. She isn't materialistic either, she patiently believes in her job and she has an amazing reputation for her passion in helping others.

Being drawn to strong women made me realise that I wanted to be like them too. So one day, just as I was starting out on my own, I wrote a list of things I valued.

1. **Be strong.** This meant I wanted specifically to be independent. I'd seen female relatives be reliant on their husbands and I didn't want that. I wanted to learn to drive my own car, earn my own money and be successful in my own right. That way, I would never need to rely on anyone else. This made me feel good.

2. **Have integrity.** I always wanted to be honest. Never two-faced or feeling the need to screw anyone over. Being loyal stems from my family too and I wanted to be that person in the wider world.

3. **Earn respect.** Women have it harder than men. We have to be a bit like a boiled egg, not too hard or too soft-boiled! We have to hit the right note. This isn't sexist, it's the reality. If we are too tough, we are called a bitch; if we're too soft, people walk over us – but there is a middle ground.

If you know what your values are, it certainly makes it easier to stick to your goals. It also makes it easier to have boundaries when you confront people or challenges.

Knowing who you are and what you believe in is a big step on the ladder!

You CAN change your mind

Now, I don't necessarily mean your goals or lane here. It's best to stick to something if you want to succeed. I mean you can change your actual mind and the way it works – and there's scientific proof about this too!

Years ago, a researcher called Carol Dweck studied thousands of kids to see why some of them succeeded and some of them failed. And what she discovered was amazing. Some kids developed a fixed mind-set, where they avoided challenges, saw effort as pointless and felt bad about the success of others. Other kids had a 'growth mind-set', where they persisted despite setbacks, learned from criticism and felt inspired by others. Carol discovered that the good news is we can actually decide to develop a growth mind-set.

Another study Carol was involved with even revealed that kids' brains grew (connected new, stronger neurons!) when they were pushed outside their comfort zones. And this can work for adults too.

Now, I'm all for sticking in one lane, but *sometimes* things just don't work out. You could find yourself on the wrong course or at the wrong university, or decide that actually you don't want to follow the path you've set yourself on.

Trust your gut on this one. I don't advocate people chopping and changing because they've hit a rut or a hurdle. But when you know deep down that something is no longer for you, there is no shame in changing your path. As long as you stick to the next one! It's then you can decide to follow a mind-set that promotes growth.

One amazing lady I spoke to called Carolina had to face some stark choices, but instead of sinking, she swam into something even better! Carolina was doing a degree in media and found herself a job in PR, the career she thought she wanted to go into. But after a couple of years she burnt out. Exhausted by the fast pace and pressure to socialise after work, Carolina decided marketing wasn't the path for her, but after so many years studying, what else was she going to do?

Often when this happens we can feel trapped by indecision and anxious about what will happen next. But I say, instead of panicking, take stock of what you want again. Make a list, daydream, and get back to who you are inside and what you want your life to look like. Remember, a fixed mind-set can be challenged and changed.

Carolina began to do this, so when an opportunity popped up she recognised it. She unexpectedly won a prize for her dissertation at university and when she collected it she had a major *Eureka* moment. Carolina decided to quit her job and become an academic. She applied to a university in Australia and did a PhD and a teaching course.

She told me: *'I definitely advise people who are not happy in their current position and life to change track if they can and know what to do. There is no point in being stuck in a life you hate. You will be worse off. And the younger you are, the more time you have to retrain.'*

How to be productive on your path

Focus on what you DO want. When things got tough for me, like when I felt out of my depth on the course, or I was tired or needed a break, I tried to look at what I was enjoying. I focused on thinking about life after university and plans I had. I focused on the good friends I'd made. If you are not happy in any area despite trying your hardest for a significant time, then there is nothing wrong with changing course. But make sure it's a path you can stick to.

Be open to learning new skills. It's easy to try to keep proving yourself, but if you don't have the actual skills to back it up, you're bound to fail and feel bad about yourself. If something isn't working out for you, then start asking: *'Why?'*

Does it mean you need to do a new training course? Or find a mentor? Or practise more? Whatever it is, a growth mind-set tells us that we need to open our minds and our hearts to what the next big step is. If you tell yourself you're stuck and have no options or cannot improve your skillset, then that will come true.

Act 'As if'. As I've said, I am not a natural student. But I acted as if I was, just like all the other geeks in the library. I turned up for lectures, I took care with my projects, I worked as hard as I could. The truth was I was interested in the subject but I needed to put in extra effort to actually pass. If I didn't understand something, I always put my hand up and asked. Even if this felt awkward at first, I soon didn't care. I had to, at first, pretend to be the most studious student before it began to feel natural to me.

Find likeminded people. Some people are drains, other people are radiators. We all know that saying. Think about how the friends you hang out with make you feel. Do you leave their company feeling stronger and confident in yourself? Or do you walk away feeling drained and questioning yourself? I had friends at school who laughed at my dream of wanting to study dentistry, so I actively avoided them. I also gravitated towards fun people at university who worked AND played hard. Life is for living, not for trying to justify yourself. Find the people who will cheer you on outside of your comfort zone too. Which brings me to my next tip…

Step out of the cosy comfort zone! We all know what this feels like. We are safe. We know it all. It's easy. It's routine. It's peaceful. This is fine for some of the time, but if you want to progress, you have to leave the zone, baby!

Don't think it's not scary for some people, because it is really scary for *everyone*. The point is, the more you try new things, the more you'll learn to cope with the fears and then the more resilient you will naturally become. Many times in my life I have felt waaaay out of my comfort zone. Starting university, trying to buy my own dental practice (I wasn't even 30 years old and I was a woman; who did I think I was?!), even going on TV for *Real Housewives* are all big examples of when I took the plunge outside the zone I felt comfy in.

Looking after number one

This isn't about being selfish or not thinking of others. It's about being in the best possible place so you can rely on and trust in your own resilience. If you don't feel good either mentally or physically, then you're not going to feel resilient.

ALL of us feel worse when we are unwell, exhausted, feeling vulnerable or even just plain hungry. If you're feeling any of these things, know your inner strength will be lowered and avoid making big decisions during these times.

To make sure I feel good, I have a few little things I stick by. I try to eat healthily and look after myself, but for me, the most important thing is to give myself time.

Time to recharge.

If you work hard, you need to learn to relax hard too. This is something I'm not always good at doing. Loads of people love to sit on the sofa with a bowl of Doritos for some Netflix and chill, but if you're a go-getter it can feel harder to 'allow' yourself the time and space. An athlete needs to give their muscles time to recover in between races, and so does everyone else, whatever they're striving for.

Surrounding yourself with positive people helps too. If you find yourself feeling drained or tested after seeing your mates, then think about who you're choosing to hang around with.

My friends are my cheerleaders. Anyone else, I just don't have time for. I learned this very early on. When I confided in others my dream of being a dentist or joining the show, I quickly realised who would support me and who wouldn't. I made a decision then and there that I wouldn't tolerate people doing me down. And neither should you.

During my downtime, I love hanging out with my mum. Being with her is like plugging in my soul battery for a quick recharge. But it could be your best friend, your boyfriend or even a work colleague during your lunch break who does it for you. If someone is interested in what you have to say and enthusiastic about your goals, and you feel uplifted after being in their presence, then seek them out when you need it.

Sometimes life is so busy we don't even ask ourselves how we are feeling. We just plough on. But occasionally stop, take a few deep breaths and really think about how your body feels. Are you tired? Feeling emotional? Do you have a niggling worry you can't rid yourself of? We all need time out to feel good or at least be aware of how we are feeling to avoid burning out completely.

Have a little patience

'Success is the sum of small efforts repeated on a daily basis.'

Not only is 'Patience' a good song from Take That, but it's a good lesson to learn. It's hard too. Because who doesn't want it all now, now, NOW?

Life today moves at such a fast pace and the reality is, we actually can have lots of things pretty instantaneously. If we want a pizza, an Indian, a new dress from Boohoo (next-day delivery!) to name but a few things, we can order it to come within minutes or hours. If we want to watch the next episode of our favourite TV show, we can just sit and binge-watch until we've had enough. If we want to meet a new boyfriend, we can arrange a date within moments on Tinder... the list goes on!

But think about it: it's not nature's way to rush anything. I love the quote 'Nature does not hurry and yet everything is accomplished' by Lao Tzu. If you think about a baby, he or she has to learn to roll, before crawling and then walking. And that's just like us when we're learning new skills.

I've been impatient all my life, and right now I'm the epitome of someone reaping the rewards of working hard in their teens and twenties – yet I had to be patient to get what I want and the life I want. It's such a key, but underrated skill and at times it's so hard to master. The good news is, it's like wine: it gets better the older you get! But for now, it's a skill to practise.

Practise patience

When it comes to something worth having, really worth having, we have to accept we'll need to practise patience to get there. Few things worth having happen overnight. Look at the lives of lottery winners, for example. One recent study showed that people who won the lottery were not any happier, and in fact many were less happy, as their lives were thrown into turmoil and their relationships were often wrecked.

Patience also helps us not to overreact or react emotionally only to regret it afterwards. It helps us not to have a knee-jerk reaction to situations.

Long-term commitment to your goal makes it much more likely you'll achieve what you want. But patience isn't about sitting back and waiting for everything to fall into our laps either. That's procrastination, where we overthink and never act. Patience means we stick to what we want to do and keep working towards the goal, day after day, however hard things get. We stay in our lane, eyes on the prize, trusting that we will get there in the end.

So what helps a person become more patient? There are a few tricks I can recommend.

Firstly I would be prepared for loads of hurdles, whatever it is you're trying to achieve. We all fantasise about getting from A to B, or to our goal, in a series of simple steps, one after another – jump, jump, jump. But the reality is, nothing ever works like that.

If you learn to expect setbacks (both big and small ones!), you're less likely to be upset by them.

When one comes up, take the time to think clearly how you'll get around it. Don't beat yourself up that it's happened. Focus on the solution instead.

Making yourself wait for something might even be out of your comfort zone at first, but delaying gratification is useful to help us exercise our patience muscle.

Even in everyday life we can improve our ability to be patient. If you're standing in a queue and it's not going down fast enough, take some deep breaths and focus on something else rather than your frustration. Being mindful of your thoughts as they happen can stop your impatience in its tracks. Little things like feeling your feet rooted firmly on the floor and taking ten very deep breaths and releasing the air slowly can help ground us. Or even using what feels like wasted time productively. Maybe reply to your text messages you've missed or run through your 'to do' list mentally. Focusing on anything except the frustration will make it melt away.

We all have impatience 'triggers'. Being stuck in traffic, waiting for a bus, our laptops taking forever to load, our phones running out of charge… those are the little things that can build up. But if we learn to adapt and be patient with the small things, we have more chance of confronting the bigger things that hit us.

There is definitely something to be said about the patience required to earn your own success and money. Without a doubt, you'll appreciate it more. You will grow as a person and as a woman will benefit from being independent. The respect you'll have for yourself will be greater than you can imagine, and when and if you fall on hard times, your resilience will kick in.

When you just want to give up

I don't like to talk about giving up. But we have to, if we want to examine what makes us resilient too. It goes back to how we have programmed our subconscious, but with all the best will in the world, events *will* conspire against us.

It's the pain barrier all of us face at one time or another.

And I mean all of us. There is not a single successful person you see or hear from who hasn't experienced The Wall of No Hope. But the difference between the person who succeeds and the one who fails is that the successful person carries on.

Before we throw in the towel, we need to look at why we had the goal in the first place and ask ourselves honestly: what can I do to change this situation around?

It happened to me after my first year of university. I worked hard, or so I thought, as well as partying hard. But then I felt the sledgehammer blow of failure when I realised I'd failed all my first-year exams. The pain of reading the results on that slip of paper will never leave me. It was as if someone had come along and snuffed out my candle completely.

I went back to my student digs in tears. I knew I had to tell my mum and dad. That was tough. But then I had to speak to myself afterwards. I knew this could either finish me off or I could take it as a massive wake-up call.

Thankfully I choose the latter.

In dental school, you have one chance to retake the exams before they throw you out, so I decided to go for it. But also I had to take stock. Where had I gone wrong? It was time to be *brutally honest* with myself. I knew I had partied too hard. I had made a great group of outgoing and likeminded friends. But now I had to drop the invites for more revision sessions. I had to swap going out on the town for the library. I had to give this my best shot.

It meant learning to set boundaries in my life. It meant learning to say no. It meant losing friends. It was painful and it felt weird, but it was a choice I had to make.

If things are not going as you wish, think about your priorities. Be honest with yourself. Could you work harder? Work smarter? If it can be done, do it.

The second major time I felt like giving up happened years later. I was working in my first dental practice job, finishing a part-time Master's degree and facing a huge breakup with my then boyfriend. We had been together for years and the pressure of work, study and heartbreak had taken its toll. Meanwhile, I was also in talks about buying the dental practice I now own.

For anyone, it was a hell of a lot to deal with. Then, just as takeover negotiations were getting somewhere, the dentist who had the most clients and was the biggest name left the practice! I heard on the grapevine: *'The practice is worthless now. It will sink.'* Talk about a knockback!

At this point it was impossible not to notice doubts creeping back in. Was I wasting my time? Was I too ambitious? Too big for my boots?

It was at this point that I took time out for myself. I went for walks on Sundays in the fresh air. I confided in Mum and my friends how I was feeling. I looked for a happy place whenever I had the opportunity. You might find it with exercise, or a meal out with your mates, or a mini-break if you can afford it. Whatever it is, do it. Give yourself a little bit of headspace and time to recover from the setbacks. Then go back to your original goal. Ask yourself, why did you want this in the first place? Do you still want it? If the answer is a simple 'yes', then you will find a way!

After a few days, I decided to plough on regardless. I had to ignore all my critics again. If every single time I faced a knockback I gave up, then there was no point trying. Besides, for me it was a prize I knew I wanted more than anything.

To own my own dental practice was something I wasn't prepared to give up on. So I kept going.

Just know that setbacks, times of despondency or even the desire to give up completely will happen! Accept that. Embrace it. And decide you will go on anyway. Dreams and goals only ever come true this way.

<u>Surviving when you want to give up</u>

1. **Take time out.** Crank up the self-care. Talk it over with a friend or your mum. Go away for a few days. Take yourself out of the situation so you can look at the problem from a new perspective.

2. **Reach out for support.** Tell your teacher, your tutor, your best friend or someone you know who's been through something similar. Don't be afraid to admit how you feel. It's not a sign of weakness to ask for help. It's very often the fastest way out of

your rut or to see life from a different perspective. The more we ask, the more we learn, and ultimately the stronger and more experienced we become.

3. **Refocus on the main goal.** See it from the long-term perspective. You might be exhausted now, but once you've regrouped, do you still want to carry on? Chances are you do.

4. **Know you're not alone.** Every single successful person has felt like you do now at some point. But there is always a way through it.

Rule 4: Don't be afraid to set BIG goals

What do you want? I mean really, really want? (If I can channel The Spice Girls, who I loved to bits when I was younger!)

I believe you should set your goals high and not be ashamed of it. After all, what's the phrase? Reach for the stars and land on the moon.

I also love this quote by Pablo Picasso: *'Our goals can only be reached through a vehicle of a plan, in which we must fervently believe, and upon which we might vigorously act. There is no other route to success.'*

On the way we all have to face our inner fears and doubts. But if you keep coming back to your imagination, picturing that person you *want* to be, you're well on your way to becoming it. I believe it's your inner wealth that will form your outer wealth.

Setting those goals

Right, so, you know what you want, but where do you start? I knew I wanted to be a dentist, so I had a clear goal and a pathway to follow. I had to study to get into university, then complete the course, then the training and then find somewhere to work. But I also had goals about other stuff in my life. These were the things I wanted:

1. To achieve a sense of contentment in what I was doing
2. To get to the top of my game in my chosen career
3. To have a family one day
4. To make a positive difference to people's lives
5. To afford a lovely home
6. To have fun while doing all the above

Not much to ask for then, is it?! But in all seriousness, I do believe that if you have a clear idea of what you want, you've more chance of getting it. After you've done your daydreaming and steeled yourself for all the ups and downs, there is no reason why you – why anyone reading this book – shouldn't get it.

We all have good brains, even if we are not naturally academic or are sometimes low on confidence. Using our brains, we can create goals and start on our paths to success.

I spoke to a Jessica Rogers, who is a Life Coach Directory member, about how you set your goals from scratch. She uses a popular method of goal-setting called SMART goals, which stands for specific, measurable, accountable, resonant and thrilling. She said: *'By following identifiable points we are much more likely to achieve our goals. This is my list I work with clients from and many of them find it very effective.'* These are her tips:

1. **Specific:** Spend time thinking about exactly what you want. Think about how things make you feel rather than just wanting material stuff. If you need to use a vision board, cut out pictures from magazines which illustrate what you want in life, especially things with an emotional attachment. Vague goals never work; a goal needs to be something you can put your finger on and be precise about.

2. **Measurable:** Write down where you are now and where you want to be and give it a score. For example, if you'd like a beach holiday and ideally you want to go to the Bahamas, that would be a 10. Ask yourself: 'How far away am I from this now?' If it's a 2, then think of realistic ways of achieving a 5. It might not be affordable to go to the Bahamas, but you could have a relaxing holiday in the sun elsewhere! Write things down. Keeping a journal of your next steps really helps.

3. **Accountable:** Look at why you want this particular goal. Is it because you need some time off or want

to spend more time with loved ones? Or do you want a holiday with a partner? When you have decided, make sure you tell someone about it. If you share your ideas, others might be able to help and you can share your progress.

4. **Resonant:** Choose goals you want deep down and can feel in your gut. You need passion to drive you forward. Think about the definite ways you can work towards it next. For example, you might need to save money for a holiday by working extra hours, or you might need an extra job to make up the cash. You might need to find friends who want to come with you.

5. **Thrilling:** Keep your journey towards your goal as interesting as possible. Decide on something which makes you want to jump out of bed in the mornings. Ask people for help if you need to. And reward yourself as you achieve small steps towards the goal.

Jessica points out that the goals need our proper attention. *'Writing things down is a first step. Referring to what you want on a regular basis and ticking off lists is a powerful tool.'*

If you don't actually set any goals, you're almost definitely going to fail in reaching them.

Celebrate the small wins

We all need little pats on the back. We all need encouragement. Doesn't matter how old or successful we become, we need to know we're doing okay.

Yes, even the people at the very top of their game need to celebrate achievements, especially if they are sacrificing other things in life for their goals.

Ever heard of the phrase *'It's all about the journey, not the destination'*? This is so true. We're never 'finished'. We might complete a goal, but ultimately things move quickly and it won't be long before another one turns up. Even when we think we have 'got there', there will be another road to take, another hurdle to face. So why not decide to have a bloody laugh along the way while you can, by deciding to celebrate those mini-wins?!

It could be that you made it through a tricky week so you treat yourself on the Friday to a takeaway or a drink with a friend. It could be that you learned a new skill, like how to change a car tyre for the first time. High five! Why not tell someone you did it and feel pleased with yourself?

Every time we allow ourselves to feel good, we get a hit of endorphins and it makes us feel even better about ourselves. Which is what we all deserve, and I mean YOU too!

Every win matters

After every single exam pass (and I have taken a lot, believe me!), I always let myself celebrate. I called my parents or friends, had an afternoon off and basked in the knowledge that it was another step on my journey. I didn't allow myself to worry about the next one until I had sat back and thought, *Well done, Hanna!*

Likewise, when I got my first pay cheque, I treated myself and one day bought my first pair of Valentino shoes. The feeling of being able to afford something myself made a lot of my sacrifices worthwhile.

I'll never forget the first time I bought a new car after years of driving old bangers around. It was an Audi TT about four years ago. Getting that car was symbolic of everything I had done up until that point. The smell of the leather, seeing my name on the little Audi plaque as I collected the keys, the glass of champagne the salesman poured me (although I couldn't drink as I was driving!)… It made me euphoric, as I'd dreamed of owning a car like that since I was a teenager. And I savoured every second of it, unashamedly.

When you succeed in what you're doing, however small, it feels good. Your self-esteem grows, along with your resilience. Your experience of the world feels more satisfying. And when the next hurdle crops up, you'll feel better about riding the storm.

Pamela Lewerenz has been a businesswoman for three decades and now runs a business consulting company, The Brick Wall Coach. She shared a great idea about how to celebrate success along the way with her 'success jar'. She told me: *'Each day I put at least one of my accomplishments into the jar. It could be a great phone call I'd had, or something major I crossed off my "to do" list. The key thing is, even if you feel you didn't do anything that day, there should always be something to put in the jar. Then at the end of the month I take all the papers out and allow myself a moment to feel good about my mini and major achievements. My treat will be to celebrate by taking some time for myself, which could be anything from sitting in my favourite coffee shop to booking a weekend away.'*

Don't feel like you need to save up your celebration until right at the very end either. Not only is this likely to make you feel despondent (who wants to wait for years and years in some cases?), but it's also not very motivating. Keeping yourself feeling fresh, inspired and energised towards your goal won't always be easy, so treats and rewards along the way are vital.

It's the symbolism that counts. It tells our subconscious we are worth it. We deserve to feel good. And when the going gets tough (which I've said it will do!), we can feel motivated to carry on.

The taste of success when you've earned it yourself

Earning your OWN stuff and paying your own way is a feeling that can't be beaten. If someone else pays for you, it's not the same. It's short-lived. The sense of achievement from working hard and earning your own dress, your own car, your own whatever it is you've bought yourself is much more satisfying.

But it's not all about materialism and splashing the cash. Happiness does not come from money. Money might give you more choices at times, and I'm all for earning your own place in the world, but contentment is something which runs much deeper than anything money can buy.

And if you're not depending on someone else to pay the rent, you'll have more freedom.

Success can mean different things to different people too. Ultimately success comes when you feel contented about what you're doing. It could be that you're a stay-at-home mum and love it. It could be that you're in a low-waged job that you gain a lot of satisfaction from. Or it could be that you're always striving for the next thing but loving the journey. Goals and success are as individual as we are.

When I was little, I used to notice other families had holiday homes, wore nicer clothes and were basically richer than us. So one day, I quizzed my dad about it.

'Dad, don't you want us to be rich too?' I asked him.

And he laughed.

'Listen, Hanna,' he said. 'I have two healthy children, a wife I love and a happy home, so that means I am the richest man in the world.'

It was then I learned that as much as it's wonderful to have nice material things, success really IS about experiencing genuine contentment with what you have. At the end of the day, our personal relationships are a huge factor in this. Your bank balance or flash car will not be by your bedside when you're sick or dying. It's the things that money cannot buy, like love, friendships and strong, satisfying bonds with people in our lives, that make us rich or successful. Losing sight of this means success might always be out of reach, whatever our bank balance says.

Step by step to the finish line

'To get through the hardest journey we need take only one step at a time, but we must keep on stepping.' – Chinese proverb

Having a specific goal in mind can help you build little steps into big ones – even if at the time it might seem like the 'big goal' is unimaginable.

Take the story of Jessica Michael, who found herself stuck in bed with ME when she was just 18 years old. Jessica had previously been fit and active, but gradually she felt worse and worse, until she couldn't even lift her head off the pillow.

People with ME have to have suffered symptoms for at least six months to a year before they can get a diagnosis, so that's a long time to suffer in silence not knowing what is wrong. By the time Jessica was 19, she finally had her official diagnosis, so she started looking into treatments.

She told me: 'Previously I had been at university, so I had to go and see if they would allow me to finish the course. Even getting out of bed and making myself go in for a day wiped me out for weeks. It was a nightmare. Doctors gave me antidepressants but I refused to take them. I wasn't depressed because I had depression, I was low because I couldn't get out of bed.'

Then Jessica watched something on TV which gave her a goal and changed her life.

She said, 'Stuck in bed, I had the telly on and I switched channels to see the London Marathon. Then it struck me. I was in my prime and laid up in bed watching the world go by, and I vowed to myself: I will run the marathon one day!'

To outsiders this goal might have seemed crazy, but it helped Jess to focus on her recovery. That's the thing with our goals – they are completely personal to us. We shouldn't be affected by what anyone else thinks or wants to do. They're for our own lives and help bring about the changes we want to see!

Thinking just one step at a time, Jessica started researching ways to help her cope with ME, looking into nutrition especially. She decided to start eating raw vegan foods, and over the next few weeks her energy levels began to improve. This built up over the next few months, so she was able to leave her bed for longer periods of time, until one day she could actually walk around the block by her house. With the image of running the marathon one day, she knew she was on the right path!

Jessica's interest in food grew, until she understood so much more about nutrition. With higher energy levels, she also slowly built up walking into learning to jog and run. Again, small, manageable goals were key to building up strength and stamina. It took four years, but aged 23, Jessica finally won a place in the London Marathon and she completed it in an amazing time of just over four hours.

Jessica said: 'It was once a goal that seemed so far-out, but it gave me a focus, a dream to build upon. Without that, I don't know what would have happened.'

As her fitness improved, so did other areas of Jessica's life. She found she had the stamina to work again and she built an online business selling vegan food whilst training as a nutritional consultant. Then she began creating and manufacturing raw vegan superfoods skincare through her company, Rawgania, which she runs today.

Phew, what a journey, but one which started with a single step.

Rule 5: Smile through Imposter Syndrome

The definition of Imposter Syndrome is when people doubt their accomplishments and feel a persistent and internalised fear of being exposed as a 'fraud'.

Even Michelle Obama admits to having Imposter Syndrome. Yep! You read that right.

In a recent interview, whilst touring for her book *Becoming* (which became the biggest-selling memoir EVER, went straight to number one and sold ten million copies), Michelle admitted she *still* doesn't always feel good enough. To an audience of girls at Elizabeth Garrett Anderson School in London, she said, *'I still have a little [bit of] Impostor Syndrome, it never goes away, that you're actually listening to me.*

'It doesn't go away, that feeling that you shouldn't take me that seriously. What do I know? I share that with you because we all have doubts in our abilities, about our power and what that power is.'

Now, if even Michelle Obama doesn't feel good enough, then that says to me it's so common that we women should rise up and talk about this.

My experience of Imposter Syndrome began when I first started working as a dentist. I began as an NHS dentist. The first day I put on my uniform and invited my first patient into the room, I could feel my heart thudding. After so many years of studying, I knew what I was doing – I had studied hard, practised hard, and I couldn't wait to get started! But now that I was here as Hanna the Dentist, I felt hot and anxious.

Who do you think you are, Hanna? said the little voice inside. For a few seconds I felt like a little girl playing dentists. Crazy, I know, especially after eight long years of study and all that training.

I pushed on through and ignored the doubts, and by the end of the day I felt good about myself again. But it happened a few times and took months to go away.

After four years working for the NHS, I took the plunge and became a private dentist. This was the next big step and, as often happens when you reach outside your comfort zone, the inner voice of doubt piped up again.

'Hanna, do you really think you can treat all these paying clients?' it said.

Once again, I took a deep breath and tried to shut the voice down. There is only one way to beat Imposter Syndrome, and that's…

Fake it until you make it

Now, I don't mean faking qualifications or knowledge; doing those things will land you in hot water. What I mean is, if you don't feel confident about a situation then pretend you do, until this feeling actually becomes real.

Changing your behaviour is a very powerful way of making things happen. Just like the Law of Attraction says that what we put out there we get back, it's the same with how we behave in everyday life.

For example, if you want people to trust in your abilities, like I did when I was starting out, then you need to behave in a highly professional manner. I took time to explain to patients the treatment they were having. I gave them an insightful rundown of their X-rays. I shared my knowledge with them until they understood everything they needed to know. That extra effort soon told them I was the expert in this field. But I had to communicate this, even if inside I felt a bit wobbly about being judged.

In every area of our lives we can implement the idea of 'faking it until you make it'. If you want more friends, then behave as if you're friendly. Smile at people, be keen to hear what they have to say. If you want to be more productive in your life but feel the days run away with you, then pretend you are productive! Make lists of things to do, cross them off, pat yourself on the back, set new goals.

How you dress is important too. Even if you're walking around with a smile on your face making long 'to do' lists, if you're slobbing around in unwashed tracksuit bottoms then nobody will take you seriously. Chances are you won't feel good either. You don't need a designer wardrobe, but you do need a clean, tidy appearance, especially at work. *'Dress for the job you want, not the job you have'* is always a great piece of advice here.

But the bottom line for faking it until you make it is having the confidence to try. Even if you feel like a fraud inside and like you have zero confidence, it's still possible to pretend you have. Walking tall into a room, smiling at people when you meet them, listening to what they say and speaking as clearly as you can… these are all little things we can do for ourselves even in our lowest moments. If we act as if we are that confident person we admire, it really does come true. Trust me!

When I found myself on a red carpet at a big ITV event for their talent alongside huge household names like Keith Lemon, Paddy McGuinness and Gemma Collins. For a few minutes I was overwhelmed with thinking, *Bloody hell, Hanna, what are YOU doing HERE?* But instead of panicking, I smiled my way through it and pretended a red carpet with cameras was my natural home. I walked with my head high, hoping nobody would notice what I was thinking inside. And I think I got away with it!

Everyone has to start somewhere. The best surgeons, dentists, musicians, singers, actors, comedians – it doesn't matter what skill you try in life, you are going to be shit at it when you begin. I saw a tweet recently that summed this up:

'*@werenotwizards: Your first podcast will be awful. Your first video will be awful. Your first article will be awful. Your first art will be awful. Your first photo will be awful. But you can't make your 50th without making your first. So get it over with, and make it.*'

We ALL feel like imposters

When I asked friends and family if they'd experienced Imposter Syndrome, I couldn't believe how many talented and accomplished women said, 'Me too!'

I believe women are not naturally as confident as men in certain situations. I'm no scientist and this is based on no particular study, but it makes sense to me that it's all about biology.

Men were hunter-gatherers while women stayed at home and nurtured their kids. Of course, modern life has moved us on, but our biological makeups haven't changed in thousands of years. So sometimes we ladies need an extra boost to help us overcome these hardwired feelings of lacking in confidence. Knowing you are not alone also helps. It doesn't even matter how far up the ladder you go, there will be someone struggling like you.

Leah, 34, suffered from Imposter Syndrome after she trained as a solicitor. She said:

'Right from the start when I began working in law I was aware of the risks involved of getting things wrong, so I suffered from constant low-level anxiety of not feeling good enough.

I tried to make up for this by overcompensating by working even harder than everyone else and taking on the jobs nobody wanted to do.

I worked for six years as a non-qualified lawyer before I qualified. Being a solicitor is one of those jobs you train for but it doesn't prepare you until you're actually doing it.

After eight years, I worked out I'd even worked around three extra years in overtime.

I think women especially have no internal compass. We don't give ourselves a break and tell ourselves we are good enough, enough times!'

Leah also points out that many women are only the first or second generation 'career' women in their families.

She said: *'Women who work are still writing the rulebooks. We are still learning. Our place in the workplace is not always a given or that comfortable, so we should help each other to feel better about belonging.'*

After burning out, Leah left the profession and set up a new mentoring business called Searching for Serenity, helping other women who struggle with similar issues she faced.

'It's something I have knowledge about because I have lived it,' she said. *'And so many women suffer in silence.'*

Stop comparing yourself

All around us we will find someone richer, smarter or more attractive than us. There will always be someone better at the job or more confident at what they're doing.

When I first joined *Real Housewives*, I found myself instantly comparing my body size and shape with the other girls'. I mean, they were all tall, beautiful gym bunnies and

I was being asked at times to get in and out of a swimming pool with them!

But I took a deep breath and did it anyway, because I reminded myself that nobody is looking at me. Everyone is far too busy worrying about themselves to notice others. This is true in most situations.

The phrase 'compare and despair' rings true here too. Every single time you look over your shoulder at someone else, you are wasting precious energy you could be using for you.

We can all feel like we are in a race. Who is going to be first to get a good job? Marry? Buy a decent house? Climb the career ladder?

Whenever we see someone achieving something we want, envy is a natural reaction.

But actually the only person we are in a race with is ourselves.

The time I reach my goals won't be on the same timeline as the next person. We are all having different experiences with different challenges and peaks and troughs. The decisions I make on my own journey have nothing to do with anyone else and we need to remind ourselves of this, sometimes on a daily basis.

Sometimes I have compared myself to others in my profession too. I have seen before and after pictures from top cosmetic dentists and felt a prick of envy. I want my work to be up there with the best of them! At a certain point looking at others who are more successful than us can inspire us. We can learn from the paths of people we see as better versions of ourselves. But ultimately if watching what other people are doing makes you feel low, anxious or bad about yourself, then it's time to stop.

There's a very fine line between being inspired by someone and negatively comparing what you are achieving alongside them. What can begin as constructive can become destructive.

Mum and businesswoman Holly Stevens told me how constantly comparing herself to other people when she worked in an office chipped away at her self-esteem.

She said: *'At first comparing myself to other people seemed helpful as I could pick up hints and tips from others. But then my need to compare myself went into overdrive. Even my "successes" started to feel like failures. Once I did really well at work but then spent all my time worrying how I was going to repeat this!'*

Poor Holly found herself trapped in a negative spiral when it came to her work. If she got praise from her boss, a nagging voice inside her then started asking why a colleague was earning more money than she was. In the end, all of her self-worth became hinged on the opinions of others.

Meanwhile (as if this wasn't enough to be dealing with!) Holly was juggling being a new mum to her then toddler daughter. One day she read a quote saying, *'The key to success as a working mother is to work like you don't have a family and parent like you don't have a job.'* No wonder she started to feel like a failure all around!

Understandably something had to give and Holly just burned out. It's at times like this that we need to click into recovery mode again and that's exactly what Holly did.

'I gave up my day job and decided to just focus on something I love just for the joy of it. I've always loved dressmaking and it was at the time Disney released the film Frozen *but their merchandise department hadn't made enough dresses for the kids who wanted one. I knocked one up for my daughter and then word spread of my skills to friends and neighbours. Before I knew it, I had orders for princess dresses and garments of all kinds!*

Completely out of the blue a viable business had started while at the same time I was "sewing" back to sanity. Doing something so calming and meditative boosted my mental health no end. I started this project with no goal in mind either, so I didn't put pressure on myself. I just went with the flow to see what happened!'

And sometimes that's all we can do. Do the thing you love if nothing else is working and see where it takes you! Today, Holly runs a successful dressmaking design business called Wowsers in Your Trousers, which started from a humble Facebook page. And finding her passion again has led to a renewal of Holly's ambition.

'I still have dreams even if I only work school hours now,' she told me. *'Designing and making Princess Charlotte's wedding dress maybe! But my dreams are no longer critical to everything I do, and I still know I'll be happy doing what I am doing on a daily basis.'*

Holly's story proves that if you stop comparing yourself to what everyone else is doing and just solely please yourself, you're more likely to end up in a happy place.

<u>Feeling like a fraud?</u>

We've all done it, from me to Michelle Obama. Imposter Syndrome is something even the most talented and capable of women have felt. If you're having a bad day and struggling with self-esteem around who you are and what you're doing, here are some thoughts to get you through it.

1. **Acknowledge that this is what you're thinking!** Realise it's not a good thing for you, and decide you're going to overcome it. Being honest is the first big step.

2. **Write down your job description.** This will help you focus on what your strengths are, but also help stop you over-servicing. A lot of people with Imposter Syndrome overcompensate by working longer hours or not having lunch breaks, or they put down what work they have achieved. By writing down an exact list of what you need to achieve in your role, you might be able to relax and refer back to it, knowing you ARE good enough!

3. **Write down an achievement or a 'win' in your job.** This helps you feel good when things are going well and signposts that YOU are good at what you do! If someone says something good about your work, then write it down and keep it. I have posted some of my thank-you letters on Instagram because I'm proud of what I've achieved and grateful for having lovely customers.

4. **Create a supportive network around you.** It seems to me that there are tons of women out there who quietly feel like frauds, so let's all shout about it and big each other up. Tell your friends and colleagues how you're feeling, start a conversation about it. None of us should suffer in silence anymore.

Rule 6: Embrace risks in your life

Without a doubt, all the successful people I've met have one thing in common: they take risks.

In my life I've taken several risks. First was telling the world I wanted to be a dentist. Some people were only too happy to knock me down, so I risked (and faced!) rejection, but I carried on regardless.

The next big risk was taking the plunge and buying my own practice near where I lived.

I was young and had no clue what I was doing. I just knew I wanted to go for it. I had to get out a big bank loan and negotiate for two whole years to buy it. This was a huge risk, both professionally and personally. I faced financial ruin if it didn't work and chances were I'd struggle to work again too.

What helped me through, once again, was my daydreaming – or in this case, visualisation. The practice I was looking to buy was in a Victorian building painted a hideous hot pink and blue, like a boudoir. It was crying out for some TLC. But every time I walked past or visited the place to discuss the takeover, I didn't notice the poor décor. Instead, I saw something different.

In my mind's eye I saw the walls outside painted a fresh, gleaming white. Inside, instead of the tired-looking waiting room with plastic chairs, I saw smart wooden floors and dark-green Chesterfield sofas where my future patients could relax while they flicked through glossy magazines. Above their heads I saw a new logo for my company, all nicely branded and making a big, impactful feature on the wall.

Even if *at that moment* I didn't have the money or even the contract to turn the practice around, I *knew* this was what I wanted to do. To the point that it felt real and very possible.

My little fantasy saw me through the tough times of the negotiations. **It helped me focus on my end goal, rather than the risks I was taking.** Arguably most things in life are a risk and dwelling on them too much would mean we'd never get anything done. We have to see the bigger picture and focus on the end goal.

Just living is a risky business... so go for it!

Falling in love is a risk (heartbreak), studying for a qualification is a risk (fear of failure), getting a new job is a risk (being sacked), even just walking out of your house and across the road is a risk! If we thought about the possible negative consequences of anything too much, we'd never do it.

And this is the key thing: you need to focus on what you want rather than what you're risking if it all goes wrong.

My husband, Martin Kinsella, has also taken risks. He set up his business doing fillers and Botox when, at the time, it wasn't very popular. He could have taken a gamble that failed. But thankfully it didn't. He focused on his desire to diversify his business, and with dedication and expertise he did it.

The next biggest risk I took in my life was to accept the offer to appear on *Real Housewives*. The call came after Martin had made an appearance on a couple of episodes and a producer wanted to meet me. After several chats they thought I'd be perfect for the show, even if at first I couldn't understand why.

Here I was, a professional running a business – I wasn't even a housewife! But I was intrigued and happy to consider it. It was everyone else around me who told me to do otherwise. Pretty much all of my family were dead against it. Many of my friends also thought I'd be crazy.

'You'll be made to look like a laughing stock,' one said.

'They will twist your words in the edits,' another warned.

'Your clients will stop coming to the practice,' someone else said.

Now, I really respect my friends and family, more than anyone in the world, but deep down I knew this was an opportunity I wanted to take up. Call it gut instinct or just curiosity about what life in the limelight might mean for me, but I decided to see it as a challenge and give it a go. People in the medical world hardly ever appear on reality TV shows, so I liked the idea of the challenge of showing viewers another way of life. Yes, it was a gamble, but I decided to go for it.

Once I'd made that decision, it felt like I had to rely on my inner resilience to face my critics. I thought of my resilience as a rain mac. I put it on, zipped it up and then let all the rain (other people's criticisms) wash off me.

Once I'd taken the plunge, that was that. We were signed up for a series of *Real Housewives* and were going to see where it took us!

Taking a calculated risk

Going on the show involved risk, but I trusted myself enough to not do anything foolish or embarrassing (well, touch wood, I haven't!). If you're thinking of taking a risk, then doing it in a logical way will minimise things going wrong.

First of all, think about the 'big thing' you want to take a risk on. Do you feel scared? If so, maybe jot down why you're feeling the fear. Stick to the facts. If you're scared because you lack confidence, ask yourself if it's Imposter Syndrome or do you genuinely need to brush up on your knowledge? If we base our decisions on logic rather than emotion, we are more likely to make better decisions.

Taking a risk doesn't mean not doing your homework or blindly jumping in. Writing a list of pros and cons can clarify your thoughts. What do you stand to gain? What do you stand to lose? Also, asking yourself this big question can help:

'What is the worst that could happen?'

Often if we're facing a risk, we think of the potentially catastrophic things which could happen. But if we look a bit closer, we find that most of this is fear based and most of our worst fears will never, ever actually happen!

If you can, find someone who has already followed this path you wish to be on. Often people are more than happy to help and share their knowledge. They can tell you about potential pitfalls, but also reassure you that the risk is worthwhile.

Another big question to ask yourself is this: *'What if I get to the end of my life and I've never tried this?'* This is all rather deep, but the things we'll regret on our deathbeds are not the things we've done but the things we didn't do. Looking back with a sense of wistfulness will feel worse than trying and it not working out.

Never feeling ready

All very well, Hanna, you might be thinking, but I am not ready yet!

Well, all I can say is, most of us, especially the successful people in life, won't have felt ready at the time they jumped either.

Unless you really have no experience whatsoever in what you want to do, or unless you need to do some major studying or gaining of qualifications beforehand, then you're as ready as you'll ever be, because NONE OF US ever feels truly ready.

Feeling 'ready' is where the unicorns and rainbows live, where everyone feels peace and contentment all day long – i.e. it's a place that doesn't exist. But accepting you won't feel comfortable or 'ready' is a big step in the right direction.

I was blown away by Nila Holden's story of saying 'yes' when she couldn't have felt less ready. Nila was a mum of two kids who lived in Luton and worked in the public sector. When she was getting married she decided to make her own wedding cake, so she went on a course to learn how to bake and discovered she absolutely LOVED it!

Previously Nila had never seen herself as a creative person; she'd pigeonholed herself, as she'd only got an E grade in her GCSE in Art. But baking and decorating cupcakes became her new hobby. Months later, when she was made redundant, her husband suggested she set up a new business.

'At first I thought it was crazy. I wasn't the sort of person to set up a business,' she told me. 'But he encouraged me to try it for six months just to see if it worked. I definitely had discovered a creative side to myself, so I thought I'd give it a go!'

Fast-forward six months and Nila was making luxury biscuits in her own kitchen. When she realised people in her hometown of Luton didn't want to pay a premium for luxury biscuits, she started selling them online.

'People said to me all the time, "Oooh, these should be sold somewhere like Fortnum & Mason, but I just laughed. That was a pipe dream,' she said.

Nila carried on, making biscuits and selling them at home, building up a social media following, all whilst looking after the kids.

Then one day in December 2013, while she was taking the kids to school, she had an email from a food buyer at Fortnum & Mason. They wanted to order a thousand of her biscuits for their stores for that Valentine's Day.

'I nearly dropped the phone. I could not believe it! There was absolutely no way I was ready. I knew nothing about margins, mark-ups, barcodes or anything to do with big business!'

But after taking a deep breath, Nila – despite not being ready at all – said YES!

'I couldn't bring myself to say no. I thought I'd just figure it all out as I went along. I was completely winging it. I had to google questions to find answers for things and pretend I knew what I was doing. Looking back, I just wasn't ready at all, but I knew the absolute basics and I couldn't say no.'

Nila's gamble paid off. She managed to make the order and her biscuits took off, selling in the high-end store. Within a couple of years the biscuits were also sold by Harrods, Disney and a major airline. She found bigger premises for production and even took on staff.

So despite not being 'ready', nothing held her back! Like Nila says, if she can do it, a mum from Luton in her kitchen who just started off using whatever she had in her cupboards, then so can you.

Today, Nila has moved on to coaching other people to bring their dream food businesses alive. Her best piece of advice for anyone who doesn't feel ready to take the plunge is this:

'We can know what we want and why we want it. But the question of "how" makes us freeze. But I say, the "how" can come later. If an opportunity comes along then commit to it and trust the "how" can be learned along the way. Your mind becomes unblocked when you start doing the process and you can ask questions and learn everything along the way.'

I would always choose yes rather than no, even if I wasn't sure in that moment if I could do it. Like Nila says, there will always be time to figure things out, and as long as you know the basics then why not fake it until you make it?!

Saying yes and learning later is a really common thing for successful people to do. Richard Branson wrote on his blog: 'Even if I have no idea where I am going or how to get there, I prefer to say yes, instead of no. Opportunity favours the bold.'

Now that's a quote to stick on your mirror!

Questions to ask yourself before taking a risk

1. **What do I want to gain from this risk?** Focusing on this answer rather than the fear will help you decide.

2. **Why don't I feel ready to take the plunge?** Is it because you need to do more preparation? Make a list of your credentials for the challenge. If it's possible to prep some more then do it, but be aware that often we never feel fully ready to take the plunge. It's human nature to want to err on the side of caution.

3. **What is the worst that could happen?** Write this down and then write the pros and cons for taking

the risk. If something genuinely terrible could happen as a result, then think up some contingency plan. If you're taking a financial gamble, would there be any way of clawing some money back? Be realistic about the worst-case scenarios. Often they are fear-based stuff that never happens.

4. **Is it possible to get what I want risk-free?** Hmm, I wonder if it's worth having then! Seriously, the answer is almost certainly no. Most things in life involve some element of risk. To be successful it's pretty much a certainty that you need to take risks, but don't let this put you off.

Rule 7: Learn to communicate (and listen properly!)

We all think we listen, but do we really? When we think about it, we often only hear what we want to hear.

When I was younger I only listened to people I thought were worth listening to. Like my cool friends, a few teachers I liked and my parents (albeit only now and again during the teenage years!). For many young people, feeling overconfident and like they 'know it all' is a rite of passage. That's how brains are wired in youth.

But as we get older we can appreciate that listening is a proper skill to be mastered, and not something just to be taken for granted.

You can only get ahead in life by learning to listen. Without good relationships nothing will be achieved. You can't get anything done in a vacuum by yourself. And even if you could, what would be the point of it if you had nobody to share it with?

I love self-reliance, and certainly don't want to just live off a man, but it's only by learning to communicate really well that we can get what we want out of this life. You need to be able to tell someone what you need and what your aims are. You need to find out who can help you and be open-minded enough to learn from others.

I had to learn to do it while studying, during work placements and when buying my business. And as a boss now, I definitely need to know how to listen to be an effective leader.

So we need to be shit hot when it comes to communicating our needs and asking for help as well as creating bonds and listening to others.

But listening is something we all take for granted and it isn't actually always easy.

Proper listening versus pretend listening

Have you ever been in a conversation with someone and you're so keen to get your point of view across that you barely hear what they're saying? Or have you been so nervous about what to say next that you're more focused on what your next opinion will be rather than hearing their turn?

We've all done it. But we miss a lot of what's important if we don't listen properly. Often we only hear what we want to hear and the chances of either learning from other people or creating deeper bonds is lost. If you look to understand someone else BEFORE you're hoping someone understands you, then you're more likely to have a successful relationship with them.

What's the difference between proper listening and pretend listening? Here are a few ideas.

Proper listening

You're not distracted. You are maintaining eye contact.

You can empathise with what the other person says, even if you don't agree with it.

You let them finish what they're saying.

Afterwards you double-check that you understand what they meant by asking relevant questions. If you didn't understand, you allow them time to re-frame it.

Pretend listening

You're distracted by what's going on around you, e.g. your phone, or by thoughts of what you need to say next.

You can't wait for them to finish, and you stay silent but offer no non-verbal signs like nodding or an empathising look.

You offer advice without it being asked for, or finish sentences because you're anticipating what they might say.

You're judging them as they speak.

Feeling under fire

But what happens when we're trying really hard to listen but feel attacked or judged or upset? I've seen this a few times on *Real Housewives*. In fact, I think sometimes some of us girls don't listen to each other at all at times. We all have big personalities and are encouraged to speak out with our opinions. I guess conflict is more fun to watch than one person patiently listening to another person!

While this is all very entertaining for a reality TV show, in life we need to behave a bit differently if we want to have successful relationships. I spoke to Abi Wright, from InspiringMargot.com, who runs workshops for women to help them improve their communication, especially at work.

She told me: *'People struggle to listen when they are attached to their point of view. It means they're in fear of not being heard or understood themselves.'*

I asked her what we should do when we feel we're not being understood, especially when we're getting upset. Something I saw and heard a few times on the show!

Abi told me: *'When we feel attacked we go into "fight or flight mode" and adrenalin starts to surge. It's really hard to stay calm or listen in these conditions, so I rely on a couple of techniques when this happens. I imagine my feet rooted to the ground, or if I am sitting, my sit bones on my chair, and take several deep breaths. I let the other person finish speaking completely before I decide how to respond. And if you respond rather than react from anger, you're more likely to be understood too.'*

Once Abi overheard a businessman talking badly about a workshop she had previously given about female empowerment. He said: *'Oh, I suppose it's a group for angry women to bitch about men.'*

Abi knew he was joking (although it's not really a good joke!) and it was exactly the sort of situation she wanted to stand up for herself in. So what did she do? If she'd been in a pub she might have told him what she thought, but in a professional work setting she needed to stay calm. She needed to implement the measures she taught others about.

'I used my technique, just for a few seconds, to allow those moments of upset to wash over me, before I said to him: "Actually I don't appreciate that comment, as there's little truth in it,"' she said.

It's good to come up with a few stock answers you can rely on in times when you've been hurt or offended. Taking time before you respond is even something you can ask for. There's no harm in saying you can't respond right now so you're going to go away and come back before you talk. Or you can thank someone for their point of view, but say you're going to have to agree to disagree.

Walking away from an argument if listening hasn't worked isn't a sign of weakness. It just makes life a whole lot easier!

Making judgements

When we're learning to listen, we also need to stop doing something else and that's make sweeping judgements.

Listening requires an open mind. Everything we hear, see or talk about is related back to us, and it really does take effort at times not to judge. What we look like or how we look at others is so powerful. Whether you like it or not, you get put in a bracket that stretches from colour and ethnicity to age and gender. I have experienced this myself when people assume I'm a dental nurse, just from what I look like.

And I'm as a guilty as anyone of making those judgements too. Once I dated a guy in London who told me he was a rapper. He was a white guy with tattoos and piercings (not the kind of guy I wanted to bring home, I thought meanly!) and I could hardly stop myself judging him straight away when we first met.

Unintelligent, silly and a bit cringe-worthy. And a bit of a bad boy...

These were just a few of the thoughts going through my mind. As he tried to talk to me I just didn't want to know, but I forced myself to listen (I think I was waiting for a friend to show up and thought, why not...). But after listening to him for a while, and even hearing him rap, I was blown away by his talent. He was a poet, a writer, and used words in a very clever way. Afterwards I agreed to go on a date with him and we dated for a while, he was amazing. Things didn't work out in the end, but ever since I've had so much respect for rappers' performances, whatever they look like.

I made judgements when I first joined the *Real Housewives* show too. When I first met Ester I quickly leaped to the conclusion that we'd have absolutely nothing in common. I thought she was a bit of a buffoon, if I'm honest. But after a few heartfelt conversations and watching how she deals with life, I was in awe of what a genuinely sweet and wonderful nature she has. Ester is one of the few people I've met with a huge heart who wears it on her sleeve. She hasn't got an agenda, a rarity in the world of reality TV.

Power of honesty

Sometimes our life circumstances can force us into listening and communicating in a different way. Often it's when we confront really hard times that we learn the art and power of listening. Take the story of Stephanie Davies. Stephanie always prided herself on being a 'private' person. She didn't go on Facebook to tell the world what was going on, and keeping her problems private came naturally.

Then in 2005, when she was just 24, Steph's life changed forever. After being involved in a car accident she noticed swelling in her leg, which turned out to be a huge grade-three cancerous tumour. Instantly her life was thrown into turmoil as she faced needing life-saving surgery. Luckily Steph was surrounded by a good network of family and friends, but she found herself communicating with them in a different way. First of all, she found herself opening up to medical staff in hospitals in a way she'd never done before.

'Suddenly I wanted to be open and honest, and I mean really honest about what my inner feelings were. I found when I opened up it helped soothe my worries and fears.

It meant communication during hard times made life easier. If I was having a bad day, I'd tell people so they'd understand what was happening, and I extended this to family and friends.'

Thankfully Steph made a full recovery, but two years later tragedy struck her life when she had a newborn baby boy who died when he was four days old. Steph and her husband, Alex, vowed to continue being honest about their feelings with each other and their families as they faced unimaginable grief.

'The more we opened up both with our families and each other, the more supported we felt. I believe it's our honesty and the relief of being listened to which has helped prevent us spiralling into depression or even splitting up, which is what happens to lots of parents who sadly lose a child. We discovered too our families welcomed the way we talked about our feelings as they wanted to share our headspace rather than worry about upsetting us.'

During these hard times Steph found herself struggling to be honest in the workplace and didn't feel listened to. So years later, when she became a general manager at Pan

European Networks in Cheshire, she decided to change the way people were listened to.

She said, *'Looking after the mental health of employees is something we know makes a difference and listening is a key part of this. I started an "open door policy" where anyone could give me the thumbs-up and ask for my time. We trained other staff in mental health first aid and even senior managers, so those who felt they had to continue to "be strong" had someone to share their thoughts with.'*

Steph says her key listening tips include: *'Don't jump in – let someone finish first. And don't be afraid of silences. That might be when someone is collecting their thoughts.'*

Steph's new ethos in her workplace has worked. Productivity is up, sickness days are down and staff morale is at an all-time high.

'Everyone has struggles in their life, but if you know you can take five minutes at work and not have to pretend nothing is the matter, then it makes such a difference. Being listened to and knowing it's safe to communicate how you feel can transform someone's mental health.'

The power of listening and being listened to can't be underestimated.

Giving time

The most precious thing in the world you can give someone is your time, and if you want to succeed in your personal relationships, then you need to be willing to give it.

As a boss in my dental practice, taking the time to listen has to be the number one attribute to have. I want to listen to everyone who works with me and for me, because I want them to know they matter. Because they do. If I can't trust and rely on them to help with my business, I have no business. They are the beating heart of my practice.

I am also genuinely interested. I talk to staff about everything in their lives, from their feelings and their families to what kind of dog they have and what can be improved in the practice. I want to know, because if someone is working for me, I want them to be happy. End of.

Spending time with people we admire is also so good for encouraging us when it comes to our goals. We make the mistake of thinking we 'always have time' for what we want out of life, but the reality is, time whizzes past. We have to consciously make time for things which are good for us, and especially our goals.

Hanging out with people who encourage us, or make us feel good, or who can help us on our way up the ladder is where focus should lie. Don't spend time with people who drain your energy or people you don't have anything in common with, or just to people-please.

If instinctively you're feeling like time is passing you by, start keeping a diary of how you spend your day. Monitor your phone to see how much time you spend on apps and start making lists of things you'd like to achieve. We all think we don't have enough 'time', but we can all make time if we choose to.

Learn to listen to those who know more than you

We all like to think we're in the 'know', but people who get ahead are those who leave their ego behind, admit they don't know everything and listen to those who do!

When I started my business there was so much I didn't know. So I asked people who did. This meant admitting my ignorance, but I didn't care. If you don't ask, you don't find out!

I spoke to other dental practice owners and learned the best option was to buy a dental practice that was already up and running. Starting from scratch was seen as the hard way to succeed.

I needed to write a business proposal for the bank before I asked them to lend me the money. *A business… what?!* was my first thought. But instead of panicking, I asked someone in the know for their guidance. Before I knew it, I had a good team of supportive people around me, friends of friends or contacts who were astute in finance or dentistry and who happily gave good advice.

Looking back, I realise I cherry-picked people to help me. I picked them solely on instinct too. If I get a good vibe from someone, I go with that gut feeling even after just a couple of minutes. It's about listening to someone's tone, noticing their body language and engaging with them on a human level.

I chose to listen to others so I could improve my own knowledge. If you want to be a success in whatever you do, it's a vital rule. Leave your own ego behind, learn to listen and don't be afraid to ask for help to climb up the ladder. There are always people out there willing to give you that hand you need.

Shutting up and listening

1. **Decide here and now to be a better listener.**
   Sounds simple, but our subconscious can absorb

these things! Think about the last few conversations you've had. How much did you hear and how much did you listen?

2. **Try to consider things from their point of view.** After you've listened, think about why they've said what they've said, why they might have that point of view.

3. **Be curious.** Curious people learn so much more in life. Think about what you're learning and listen hard so you can understand. Make that your priority, rather than jumping to conclusions.

4. **Find it within yourself to genuinely care.** Nothing can beat a sense of authenticity when someone is really listening, really caring about what someone is saying. Even if at first you think it's not in your interests to listen, do it with a sense of sincerity. You'll feel better for it too.

Rule 8: Know what's real and what isn't

Let's all be real here for a second. Most of what we see on TV, in magazine photos and on social media (like Instagram!) is a glamorous version of real life. We forget this, even I forget this, but it's so important to acknowledge it.

When I first joined *Real Housewives*, it really opened my eyes to what life is like for a celebrity. Not that I see myself as one (yet!), but what you see behind the camera opens your eyes somewhat.

The first time I went on camera I insisted on doing my own makeup and hair. I slapped on my usual products and scrunched my curls with a bit of mousse. After all, I'd been doing it for years myself, so why did I need anyone to help? But watching myself back I cringed, because I looked totally washed out.

Now it takes around an hour and a half to get my hair and makeup done by professional makeup artists who have years of experience using top-quality products. I definitely don't wake up looking like I do on the show!

The biggest wake-up call for me, however, is what happens on social media. The fakery behind every carefully curated picture is something even I've found myself getting sucked in to from time to time.

The camera DOES lie

Before I went on *Real Housewives* I only had a couple of hundred followers and I'd just post every now and again when I was on holiday or maybe on a night out. If I got a few likes, it always made me smile, but ultimately I didn't spend too much time thinking about it.

But then my follower count skyrocketed to over 40,000 after my first appearance on the show. Suddenly *thousands* of people I didn't know were following me, so I felt a bit of pressure to make my Instafeed a bit more interesting. And of course, I felt I wanted to look good then too.

So I bought a selfie circle light for when I took photos of myself on my iPhone. This makes your eyes look brighter and bigger. But then I found myself taking shots and deleting them before I posted. Suddenly I felt self-conscious and critical about how I looked. Before I knew it, I found myself looking for likes and approval!

It's a scientific fact that our brains respond to the hit of endorphins every time we get a 'like' on social media. In fact, the likes are even in the colour red because that's what our brains respond to the most. Amazing, isn't it? We are chemically wired to crave a 'like' from a stranger, which takes a millisecond to do.

Now I call Instagram, 'The Instamonster'.

Because Instagram, aka The Monster, is never, ever full and satisfied. We crave the likes to feed The Monster and for split seconds we can feel better about ourselves, before we quickly feel the craving for the next 'like' and the next one and the next…

Without being aware of this, it's very easy to get sucked into the Instamonster. Recently I was out having dinner with my family in Victors restaurant in Cheshire and on a table near us we spotted a couple of reality stars. Throughout the entire meal, from starter to dessert, the girls were either taking snapshots of themselves or had their heads buried in their phones.

It made me feel so sad. These girls weren't talking to each other because they were too busy chasing likes online. They were ignoring what was happening in real life because they were so engrossed in a fake online world.

But receiving a red dot 'like' from a stranger for a photo is absolutely no substitute for proper conversation and feeling a bond with another human being. And it never will be.

We have to acknowledge that the endorphin kick is addictive and stop ourselves allowing it to control our lives. If the Instamonster is never full or happy, neither will we be.

Coming clean about my posts

While writing this book, I was scrolling through my own Instagram account and thinking about when my own camera has lied. Or when I have retaken the same picture over and over again to make life look better than it really is!

I want to admit to this, to show everyone, whoever you are, that we are all vulnerable to feeling this way. We all want to come across as better looking, happier, having more fun than perhaps we do in reality.

And the more of us who do it, the more pressure there is for others to join in.

While it's true I do work as a dentist and do love my life (mainly!), I'm not showing off the bad bits either. Like when I'm knackered, overtired and pissed off, or having a bad day. That's because I don't think that's what people want to see. Instagram has created a world where we only see the lovely parts, so to do something different seems rebellious.

But let me admit here and now: behind the scenes of some of those super-glam shots a very different story is occurring! Here's an example.

In one Instaphoto I am posing on a tree swing while on holiday in the Maldives with Martin. A while back when I was relatively new on the show we were lucky enough to stay at the luxury all-inclusive Ozen Resort and it was absolutely idyllic.

So when I spotted the swing, I spotted the chance for a photo opportunity. After handing Martin my phone to take a shot, I jumped on and asked him to get a nice Instapic. I was wearing a lovely turquoise printed dress by Sophia Alexia and a pair of white wedge shoes from Kurt Geiger, so I wanted to @ them too.

But after a minute or two of Martin trying, I started to lose patience. In every single shot he took I was pulling a silly face or my thighs looked big at a strange angle. (Maybe they didn't really, but I've always had a thing about my legs. They are bigger than the rest of me and I hate wearing bikinis or short shorts.) Because the swing was moving, the motion meant I just couldn't get the carefree glam shot I wanted!

After persevering in the blistering heat, Martin showed me more shots he'd taken. *'Come on, Hanna, there has to be one good one in there!'* he said, exasperated.

But I still didn't like any of them, so I handed him back the phone. To me this was a beautiful background and I *knew* I could look better.

'Try again, Martin!' I cried.

After a few more minutes and God knows how many shots, Martin finally got The One. In this pic I am smiling in exactly the carefree way I envisaged the first time, even though neither of us felt particularly carefree by the end of it!

Afterwards Martin flopped onto the soft white sand, red faced and annoyed.

'C'mon, Hanna. I didn't come all this way to be taking photo after photo of you,' he said. *'Can't we just relax and enjoy ourselves?'*

'It's not that bad,' I laughed, feeling a bit embarrassed I'd pushed him so far. *'It's just Instagram...'*

'Exactly!' he said, before storming off back to the hotel.

And so, you see, that one idyllic-looking shot caused a big barney between us on our lovely holiday. It got over 800 likes, but deep down if I'm honest with you those few minutes are not a happy memory when I look at that photo now.

There are many more I could tell you the honest truth about too!

The lies that live on

Antonina Mamzenko is a family photojournalist who ran her own challenge to encourage mums (and herself!) to embrace what real life really looks like. She wants to encourage others to embrace imperfection because, she argues, chasing perfectionism is stopping people recording real memories.

Her advice to people is this, **'Stop comparing your behind-the-scenes to everyone else's showreel!'**

Quite rightly, Antonina points out that we might KNOW logically that a lot of photos are filtered or doctored to make them look better, but emotionally we forget this. After all, we are programmed to believe what we see. But the truth is, in today's world of social media we need to question it.

Antonina told me, *'You just never really know what's happening behind the scenes, so never make the assumptions when you see a photo. Someone apparently living their best life could be going through a health scare or family troubles. The perfect-looking house was probably tidied up just for the photo shoot and doesn't look like that any other day of the year. Your friend's children might look like they are gracefully running into the sunset, but what you don't see is the meltdown that preceded that idyllic picture.*

The only way to deal with it is to learn to ignore it. Stop looking at Instagram posts every day. Or at least remind yourself: "Everything I am seeing has another story behind it."

I have met mums who have told me they are not ready to have their pictures taken because they want to lose weight or get their hair done or wear something different. Of course there is a time and a place for looking and feeling good, but we should live in the moment when we're creating those memories to keep. Our kids think we are the most beautiful people in the world. I look back at my own albums where I wish I had more photographs of my mum and dad when they were my age – and I don't care if their hair looked perfect or if they were wearing their Sunday best.'

This is a big wake-up call, isn't it? While we're all chasing perfection, maybe we should think about what memories we are *really* leaving behind?

Keeping sane using social media

The subject of remaining sane using social media could make a whole book in itself. I'm a 33-year-old professional dentist who recently found herself thrust into the limelight and even I've struggled to adjust, so I know how hard it must be for younger women.

A sense of perspective is vital. You'll never get real satisfaction from social media, so by all means use it, but know there's a real world out there that needs you to be present in it too. Not buried in your phone, not messing around with an app to make your legs longer or eyes bigger, not chasing likes from strangers. I've used filters before but draw the line at doctoring my photos. I am who I am.

Genuine memories don't need doctoring. You're never going to look back at a lovely memory and wish you had spent more time editing it, I promise. You are never going to be younger than you are now. In ten years' time I can guarantee you'll probably look back and think you look youthful and amazing.

Remember too, in 50 years' time when your loved ones look back at pictures of you, they won't be wondering why you didn't use a certain filter to look thinner or with clearer skin. They will just see memories of the person they loved. And that person is the real you, warts and all!

When I see photos of my mum at around my age, laughing in the moment with her children without a care in the world, I know this is what life is *really* about. Being authentic, being present, being who you are. It's about feeling the feeling as it happens and not trying to capture everything through a lens to control the narrative.

The biggest stories of life will be the ones we keep as memories we can still see when we close our eyes.

Tips to control the social media monster

1. **Find out what you're wasting your time on.** You can do this on your phone by tapping the settings then the battery section. It will show you and might shock you! Once you know how long you're

spending on an app, you can see what you're really addicted to.

2. **Get help.** You can download apps to limit the amount of time you use on social media, like Offtime or Moment or Flipd. Or you could just delete them off your phone and only use them online for a set amount of time.

3. **Ask yourself how it makes you feel when you're using it.** See how long you spend on it for just one day. Make a note of it. Then ask yourself: How do I feel now? Endless scrolling can leave us feeling empty, tired, demoralised… if it's not making you feel good then STOP!

4. **Find the real person behind the post.** One of the joys of social media is getting to know other people in real life too. Decide to engage with other people more – take an interest in what they're doing. Above all, remember that if a post made you feel bad (envious, upset, inadequate), tell yourself: 'It's never the whole story!'

5. **Try to live in the present moment.** Don't just live via a camera phone. Think about how different you feel when you're not worrying about getting the right shot or angle, but just seeing with your naked

eye. There's something more powerful about being fully present rather than worrying about capturing a shot for social media.

Rule 9: Harness your female power AND lead the way!

Embrace your femininity (and if you want to wear an eyeliner flick, wear an eyeliner flick!)

'I am very definitely a woman and I enjoy it.' – Marilyn Monroe

When I was a little girl I was obsessed with Marilyn Monroe. To me she was the perfect example of a beautiful woman. I loved her blonde hair, blue eyes and big red lips. I vowed one day to swap my curly dark hair for a mane of peroxide blonde to swish around while I wore a dress just like hers.

It took me years to appreciate the way I actually look. It's partly because since the beauty industry took off in the 1940s advertisers have sold the idea that blonde hair and blue eyes is the standard of what 'beauty' means.

I felt like an ugly duckling for a long time with my darkish skin, wild curly hair and brown eyes – oh, and don't forget the monobrow! I nagged my parents for years to allow me to pluck it. To them, plucking eyebrows was somehow a rite of passage in growing up, so it took them ages to let me do it.

The change came for me at age 16. One summer all my puppy fat melted away, I got a tan from a family holiday in Greece and I was allowed to pluck those dreaded brows. Back home, for the first time in my life boys noticed me and it felt good.

But being attractive to other people really does have to start within. Even the most beautiful women in the world have struggled with their self-image. Angelina Jolie once said, *'I am odd looking. Sometimes I think I look like a funny muppet.'* And as humbling as this, it also proves we all have different perceptions of ourselves.

I am only five foot two and a half (that half is very important!) so I've always been one of the shortest people in the room. My body shape is naturally slightly pear-shaped too, with my weight carried on my thighs. It doesn't matter how much I work out or diet, I'll never have thin, long legs. I've been a classic yo-yo dieter at times too.

Being on *Real Housewives* around tall, glamorous women has naturally made me feel more critical about my own looks. I am aware how pointless it is to compare yourself to other people, but it's hard not to do it.

The world makes women question themselves

The point is, we ALL have something we don't like about ourselves. It's human nature. But women are brought up to question ourselves in ways men are not.

This tweet summed this up for me:

@OhNoSheTwitnt

Ads for women: Be thin, be thick, love your body, your boobs look bigger in this, dye your hair, embrace your grays, these pants are slimming, be feminine, wear makeup, look natural...

Ads for men: TRY OUR BODY SPRAY IN 2 NEW SCENTS! FIERCE SHARK ABS AND BIG LION DICK!

Not only did this make me laugh but it's an accurate portrayal of society's expectations. Women have a whole raft of advertising aimed at them, subtly (or not so subtly!) making them constantly feel not good enough, especially when it comes to their looks. From the tops of our heads (hair needs shampoo, conditioner, masks, dyeing, straightening, de-frizzing... it's endless!) to our toes (are your feet 'summer ready' anyone?), we are bombarded with images of perfection, and often it's unattainable. There's a beauty product on the shelf for virtually every single part of our bodies, from our split ends to the tips of our toes. And while I love the occasional pamper session, I don't want to be made to feel not good enough, like advertising suggests all the time. It's all about making money and it's not good for our psyche.

Look at what is aimed at men and you'll see the market is far smaller. While men feel increasing pressure to look a certain way (I don't deny this is true, although it's not on the same scale as it is for women), the focus of most marketing and the world at large is on the flaws of us ladies.

Beauty will only get you so far

When I'm in the mood, I like dressing up and feeling feminine because it's fun. I enjoy having my hair done, trying new makeup and putting on a pair of heels, because it makes me feel good about myself.

But dressing up like a glamour puss isn't the ONLY thing I want out of life.

As I grew up, I realised this meant working hard and being independent *as well as* enjoying myself as a lady who wore heels and loved her wardrobe full of dresses. Dresses I've earned myself!

We need to rely on our brains to get what we want. It's your brain which will propel you into doing and being what you want to do and be. Finding your inner strength, deciding on your goals and having the balls to follow it through is what helps you reap rewards in life.

But women have to be prepared to be judged and learn how to deal with it. If you are a woman who takes pride in her appearance, people will leap to conclusions about you. And I'm not the only one this happens to.

A study in America revealed that female scientists who looked feminine (e.g. they had longer hair or wore makeup) were assumed NOT to be scientists when people were asked to make a judgement. In fact, any woman working in a male environment can find herself judged on her looks.

Knowledge puts sexism in its place

I'm young and female, so at work I experience sexism on a regular basis. Especially when I meet middle-aged male clients, I often get comments like:

'Oh, are you the nurse?'
'Are you sure you know what you're doing?'
'When did you leave school then?'

There is only one way of dealing with this. It's to be as nice and polite as possible, and then kill them with your knowledge! When clients doubt my ability, I like to sit them up in the dentist's chair and then ask them what they would like to know or if they have any questions. Then I set about answering them as carefully and with as much knowledge as possible. I will pull up their X-rays and go through things as clearly as I can and in a way nobody will have ever done for them before!

Showing your skillset can change someone's perception of you very quickly. The aim is to turn things around, so they see you differently. Yes, it shouldn't always have to be that way, but I enjoy talking to patients anyway. Often they will thank me afterwards too. Not many dentists take the time and energy to explain things as thoroughly as I do.

All over the country, there are amazing women doing jobs traditionally done by men and being very successful when they do so. Claudia Hearne was born into a family of four generations of builders and she decided to go into the industry herself. Now she runs Hearne House, a London-based design and build company that specialises in bespoke property interior refurbishments.

By the age of 23, Claudia found herself visiting construction sites and making planning decisions in a world full of men, but nothing put her off. In fact, she loves dressing up to look glam and wouldn't be seen dead without her makeup at work.

She told me: *'Yes, there is a physical side to the building industry – as a woman I wouldn't have the strength to pick up a heavy piece of steel like many of the men do – but when it comes to every other aspect of the building industry I feel completely equal. I occasionally get some shocked reactions, which can be amusing. Once I was wolf-whistled on the way to a building site and the look on the builder's face when he realised I was his boss was priceless! I love fashion and beauty, regularly having my hair and nails done, and having a job like this doesn't stop me.'*

Good on you, Claudia! It can take balls to stand up and be counted in a male world, but more and more women these days are doing so.

Despite all of this, Claudia says she still occasionally experiences sexist attitudes. Especially when dealing with tradespeople.

She said: *'I have been in this industry for several years and my husband joined the property world much later than me. But if we go to a building site meeting together, the conversations about structural and practical elements of the project are often directed towards him. Yes,*

construction sites can be sexist, but I don't get upset by it –
it just encourages me to perform even better at my job and
surprise people who make a quick judgement based on the
way I look.'

Claudia is proof that nothing needs to hold us back; she can do the job as well as anybody else, regardless of gender.

The joke's on them

Without a doubt, sexism is everywhere, but don't dwell on it. Make a joke and move on. When I asked some brilliant women to share their best phrases and stories of comebacks, they were hilarious (and sometimes very cheeky!).

'Once, when I was about 18, I attended a family wedding and this man came over and said, "God you've grown," whilst addressing my chest. I looked down at his crotch and replied, "Well, you haven't," and my dad roared with laughter. The bloke just stared at us all and walked off.'

'If a bloke shouts out, "Sit on my face, love," I always respond with, "Why? Is your nose bigger than your dick?"'

'When guys send me a dick pic on dating sites I send them back a number for child protection services, because someone has just sent me a boy's penis.'

'Once when I was living in Paris I was in a department store and some guys started making sex noises at me, so I turned around and said in French, "Keep making those noises because it's the only time you'll ever hear them," and I got a round of a applause from the women working in the wine section.'

'My mum was flashed on a train once. The guy was sitting opposite her in the summer and let his bits just flop out. She looked him square in the eye and simply said, "Is that it?" Apparently he made a very swift exit afterwards.'

How to deal with sexism

1. **Make it a big joke.** If I get catcalled in the street, I always cheer and wave back. I make a joke out of it. If you do this, it disarms the guys and they don't know where to look! They are trying to enhance their masculinity by belittling your femininity, so don't let them do it.

2. **Have a few lines up your sleeve.** Think of a few good comeback one-liners. We've all felt tongue-tied in the moment and then wished we'd said something afterwards, so there's no harm in learning a few comeback phrases beforehand.

3. **Knowledge is power.** In a professional setting, don't be afraid to show off your knowledge. Sometimes older people and very often men question younger women openly and it's fine to answer their questions. If they are making assumptions about you, then it's time to reveal how much you really know.

4. **Don't let it stop you.** There's been sexism since the start of time, but don't focus on the inequality, just act 'as if' and move beyond the crude jokes and judgements. Don't forget, many of us are only the first or second generation of women who are chasing professional careers, so see yourself as a trailblazer. One day you will be able to impart all your knowledge to your daughters and the next generation. I love to do this already.

If you want to lead, lead by example

'I know of no single formula for success. But over the years I have observed that some attributes of leadership are universal and are often about finding ways of encouraging people to combine their efforts, their talents, their insights, their enthusiasm and their inspiration to work together.' – Queen Elizabeth II

Like I mentioned, I love the Queen, especially for her leadership qualities. She is stable and humble, and I think she genuinely cares when she listens.

I think many successful women, especially leaders, don't dwell on what they're 'up against' in terms of the inequality in society or potential sexism. I think the best leaders just get on with the job in hand and take things as they come.

When I became the boss of my new dental practice I had little experience with leadership, but decided to be myself and show my true feelings towards my staff. And my main attribute is, like I've mentioned, I care.

I know I need to keep learning too. Humility is a very underrated quality. There is nothing weak about remaining humble, however high up the ladder you climb. None of us can ever say 'I know it all now', as there is always something new available – a new product, a new skill, a new way forward. And if we stay humble, we're far more likely to open our minds to recognising it.

Reaching the heights

In 2018, I finally took over the Kiln Lane Dental Practice and became owner and principal dentist. The very first thing I did was set about redecorating the place.

Then, on that first day as I walked into work, admiring the freshly painted white walls and the logo above the Chesterfield sofas I'd chosen, I wanted to pinch myself.

Once again, I knew dreams DO come true!

But this was a baptism of fire, because I had to quickly learn how to lead. Straight away I learned the importance of delegation and trusting my staff. Thankfully I had a talented and capable manager, Jo, who was able to help and tell me everything I needed to know! She was even very honest at times, explaining that I needed to be clearer in what I wanted from people rather than just barking orders.

But ultimately it was up to me to set the tone for how the business would work. My priority was that my staff would feel like a team working together who loved their jobs. Happy staff make a happy business.

Communication was key to this. If something wasn't right, it needed addressing. I had to learn to speak honestly but sensitively, a learned behaviour. I wanted staff to tell me what needed changing too, so we could all play a part in keeping things running smoothly.

This was a real learning curve for me, and I had to put my ego aside and listen to other people, like Jo. I never asked anyone to do a job I didn't know how to do myself, so I quickly learned what everyone's role was too.

Today I'm proud of my team and my staff. They make the business work as much as I do, if not even more.

Top of the game

Can you imagine finding yourself running a football team at the age of 30? Well, this is what happened to Carolyn Radford, who is the CEO of Mansfield Town FC. She talked to me about her experiences, not only being put in the spotlight in a very male-orientated field, but also facing the challenge head on as an unashamedly glamorous woman.

Carolyn said, *'I think the leadership skills I have acquired, I have gained them throughout my life. It's taken me years to hone them, so I can be true to myself, embracing my feminine side, but also be successful at my job. Being kind and feminine is possible as well as being efficient at your job and knowledgeable. You don't have to be a "bitch" in business to do a good job.*

Ultimately whatever doubts people have at first, as soon as I start talking they have to respect my knowledge – because I do know what I am talking about.

The football industry can be a nasty one. I've been looked up and down before boardroom meetings because I am a woman and because I love fashion and looking good. Early on in my career I tried to dress in power suits but gave up as I didn't feel like me.

I don't dress provocatively, I dress appropriately, but I also like to look and feel glamorous. How you dress shows respect for yourself and is something I always note when I am interviewing people.

People have underestimated me as a woman too. They have preconceived ideas that it's really my husband making the decisions or that I don't know what I am doing, but I have learned to use this to my advantage in negotiations. They soon find out they've not got the upper hand in the end.

I'm my true self at work but have learned to be a mixture of approachable and friendly, but often with new

129

players I am hard and then soften up. Putting a team together is about dealing with human beings with all the variables this brings. I think the football industry is missing a trick not having more women as CEOs because women can ask questions men would struggle with.

I deal with footballers as human beings. We want our team to win and if anyone is not playing to the best of their ability due to personal issues I want to be approachable. I need to be able to negotiate good terms of business but also have a team who perform well week in and week out.'

Carolyn's tips on being a lady boss

1. **Be your true self, even as a leader.** If you're not authentic, you won't be able to keep up that persona. Being authentic is key to communicating effectively with people, especially during tough conversations.

2. **Don't lose your feminine side.** You can be kind and nurturing as well as the boss. People perform better if they are encouraged rather than told off.

3. **Work hard.** Hard work always, always pays off.

4. **Find your resilience.** Especially in a male-dominated industry – you will need it. But don't let

it dominate your thinking. There is nothing you cannot do.

5. **Don't stop believing in education.** Keep on learning. There is always more to learn, but also seek a firm base to begin with. You don't need to be good at everything, but find something you are good at and enjoy and work hard at it.

Rule 10: Find your tribe

I've been lucky to have two pillars in my life, my mum and my dad. From an early age, my dad told me I could do anything I wanted to do. It was such a powerful message that set me up to believe anything is possible.

I have also collected a fabulous bunch of female friends from school onwards. I call them my 'cherry-picked' group. They are all smart women with interesting careers, from being a registrar cardiologist to working in the food industry for Cadbury – or, as I like to say, they have 'books and looks'. We can talk for hours about every topic under the sun or we can party in Ibiza. I met some of them at university and others are from school. Having a friendship group to do both with is such a blessing.

I think every woman needs to find her tribe. If you're lucky enough to have a good family behind you, that's amazing, but many of us are not, so a tribe on our side is vital.

Because the fact is, we NEED other people.

Even if we think we can achieve what we want alone, it's not true. There are so many people who can help us on our way. Our teachers, our mentors, our work experience colleagues, our friends, our friends' parents, online support groups... the list is endless. Yes, we need to rely on ourselves, but ultimately we need other people in the mix as we start to succeed and especially as we climb the ladder.

I have spoken to women from all walks of life who have found support when they have looked for it. Sometimes it's in really unexpected places too.

Take Kerrie's story. Kerrie is in her twenties and has cerebral palsy, which means she uses a wheelchair and can't get out and about easily like most people in the city of Bristol where she lives. She felt isolated and found it hard to make friends. But instead of moping around, she got online to use Twitter to talk about her other passions in life, mainly writing and musical theatre. By sharing her thoughts on social media, she started to make new connections. This led to arrangements to meet for a West End show. Before she knew it, she was out and about and making genuine new friends and had found her tribe!

Anushka Fernando from Surrey even found her tribe through her sick dog. She had a pug called Bertie who needed a spinal op when he was a puppy so he missed out on normal socialising. Anushka herself also struggled with anxiety at times, and being coped up with her little dog wasn't helping her either. So she took the plunge and decided to see if she could set up a little dog-walking group for pugs in her local area. To her amazement the idea proved popular and around 50 dogs and their owners turned up. Within a few months this number quadrupled! And enjoying the new boost to her social life, Anushka organised a summer party.

From there she asked a local cafe to host another 'pug' event and this gradually turned into the opening of a Pug Cafe, where owners could come but also visitors without dogs could drop in. Without her realising it, Anushka had set up her own business called Pug Cafe and found a whole community of likeminded people. Under Pug Cafe she also hosts events for Dachshunds, Frenchies, Pomeranians and more – each growing their own communities.

Anushka said, *'I had no idea something so small could end up so popular. It's completely changed my life. I gave up my job as a content writer to run the Pug Cafes and we have opened them all over London and the South East. We are not limited to the South East – we have been all over the UK! Previously I was chasing a certain kind of lifestyle but now my job and tribe come together. Thanks to getting Bertie, my sociable little dog, I have more friends and acquaintances than I could have ever dreamed of!'*

Support other women

There is nothing more empowering to a woman than hearing the stories of achievements of other women. Often it goes against our natures to speak up and talk about our talents. We can be accused of showing off, or not being ladylike, but I say if you're talented and have something to say then shout it from the rooftops!

A while back I was invited to be on a panel at a Boss Lady event in Manchester, where a group of inspirational speakers were brought together to share their stories. They included women who had achieved remarkable things.

Of course it's at times like this that Imposter Syndrome rears its head, but like always I squared my shoulders and reminded myself I was there for a reason. Not just for *Real Housewives* but also for my work in the community as a medical professional.

I know I'm not the average *Real Housewives* sort. That's why I was offered the opportunity to be on the show.

It's true I've not always fitted in with the other girls, as I like to talk problems through calmly and be articulate rather than just getting cross for the cameras. But at the same time, dentists don't often get the chance to mix with the celebrity world and I wanted to show viewers that there is another way of living. You can use your brain as well as your looks! You can be independent as a woman, having a career in medicine, and still have fun too!

Anyway, here I was at Boss Lady, when I met a fantastic woman called Misba Khan and we had a little chat before the panel.

'What do you do?' I asked her as a conversation opener.

'I went on an expedition,' she smiled.

At the time I can't say I was hugely impressed because she made it sound very humble, but when I heard her speaking on stage I was blown away. Misba represented the UK as part of an international team of women from across Europe and the Middle East on the Women's Euro-Arabian North Pole Expedition 2018, to ski across the North Pole in April 2018. And they were all mainly novices too! The concept of the trip was to improve relationships between women from differing cultures, as well as to inspire women everywhere. The unique challenges Misba faced included extreme temperatures, hunger and incredibly harsh conditions. This was a feat of survival and all of the women had to confront their own pain barriers in order to get through.

I couldn't believe Misba's physical strength and the courage she must have needed. She was a petite 50-

something woman who was brave but so down-to-earth with it. She made me realise how deeply I admire women who possess hidden talents. Then, with a quiet humility, they return to inspire us all.

Tribes of all kinds

There's no need to just stick with one tribe either. Different tribes for different things can enrich our lives in every area. I have my 'cherry-picked' girl-friends from university and school, I have professional work colleagues I hang out with, and of course I have the *Real Housewives* girls.

Mum and PR guru Holly Pither agrees. She even called her new company Tribe PR because she believes so strongly in having different friendship and support circles in her life.

She told me she never realised how important having different tribes in her life was until she became a working mum.

She said, *'I guess I had heard of the term before and the phrase "it takes a village", but I never really quite got it until I became a mum myself. Since then I have relished the opportunity to be part of multiple tribes: working mum tribes, blogger tribes and even tribes of likeminded business owners and creatives. Without this support network I don't know where I would be, especially when it comes to motherhood. There is nothing like someone simply understanding where you are coming from and what you are dealing with. And they don't need to be close by, in fact they could be the other side of the world, but just knowing someone has your back and is there for you means the world. One such instance was when my baby was suffering with reflux and I was beside myself as I couldn't breastfeed my baby. It was horrendous. But through my blog I was able to open up, meet others in a similar position and in so doing, help myself get through a really tricky time. I don't know how I would have coped without the tribe.'*

If you're looking for a tribe, you're looking for likeminded people you can empathise with and be honest with about what's going on in your life. Holly knows she gets on best with mums who feel ambitious as well as love motherhood. She said, *'I look to connect with mums who are willing to admit it's okay to love your career and your baby and that neither should have to suffer for you to follow your dreams.'* With her business tribes Holly likes to find people with ambition who are also supportive. *'I like*

*people who aren't too proud to say they need help and who
are willing to celebrate each other's success.'*

<u>Recognising the toxic tribe</u>

There is not a single woman out there I know who hasn't at some point in her lifetime fallen for a bad boy or girl for that matter. But if you find your boyfriend, friend, partner or even your husband isn't on your side, then finding your own contentment and success will prove impossible.

Years ago I had a boyfriend who showered me with love and affection for the first few months, but after I fell head over heels for him he started to criticise me until I found myself filled with self-doubt. He also quickly isolated me from friends and family, something I didn't realise was happening until months down the line. Thankfully I found the strength to leave and start again.

Real love doesn't hurt. A real partner won't want to knock you down. Everyone deserves someone who builds them up, supports their decisions and makes them feel good about themselves. If your boyfriend or partner is not doing this, it's time to look for help to escape them.

It's not always easy to recognise when you're part of a toxic tribe, be it a bad boyfriend or friendship group. Often things creep up gradually, and before you know it, you're in too deep. But at the end of the day if someone doesn't make you feel good about yourself, it means *they* are no good.

Luckily I escaped from my rubbish relationship and met Martin Kinsella in 2016. We had known each other at university, but when we got together later in life we knew we were made for each other. A big part of this is because Martin supports me wholeheartedly in whatever I want to achieve. He is my cheerleader, my coach, my best friend, and at the end of every day (however good or bad it is) he is someone I can come home to and know he's on my side. We all deserve this, and if you feel you do not, then it's time to reassess what's happening in your life.

Find a tribe to be on your side and you'll always be further down the path to whatever success you long for.

The importance of giving back

Have you ever done someone a favour for no other reason than to be kind? Feels great, doesn't it? I believe doing stuff for others is the most incredible way of earning the feel-good factor and it really does make the world a nicer place.

You might also find a tribe whilst you're doing it.

When I was at university I did a four-week placement in Africa, working in Tanzania. Two weeks were spent in hospital and two weeks in a village. What an eye-opener this was.

I saw levels of poverty I had never even read about. I saw people having teeth pulled out with little or no anaesthetic (if they run out of drugs there, it's tough luck!). I saw people with untreated cancer growing out of their faces.

I noticed some of the villagers looked at me with a strange expression too. As if they were curious about me and my life, because white people were so rarely seen. I imagined they were thinking about the privileges I had. This was something I was barely aware of until I went abroad and saw what real poverty is.

But whilst they were curious about me, I was overwhelmed by them, especially their immense generosity of spirit. They had so few material items but were so content. I stayed with a family with several children. One was a cheerful little girl with cornrows in her hair and she was so proud of her doll, which was a simple bamboo stick with a frayed end for hair and a smiley face drawn upon it.

Her giggle was infectious, and despite having so little, she had so much love in her world.

I met villagers who all happily congregated in our mud hut house every night, because my family owned the only TV. They were a community who believed in sharing, in team spirit and equality.

By the end of my four-week stint I knew my life had changed forever. Unless you go and see other parts of the world and immerse yourself in other cultures, it's easy to become blinkered about what life is about. In the West we live spoiled lives in many ways, often worrying about material things and status. Seeing people who have so little living so happily was awe-inspiring. And this made me realise where the real values in life lie.

Be open-minded

Being open to new opportunities can make all the difference to our life experience. This includes giving someone we meet a chance. We all get hung up on judgements of other people or dismiss something as 'not really our thing'.

I discovered this a few years ago when I accidentally stumbled across new friendships in an old people's home, of all places. I was living in a flat share and had a note to say my new mattress had been delivered to the local old people's home by accident, so I found myself knocking on the door there.

After being invited inside, I was hit by the heady scent of Werther's Originals and wool for knitting.

Oh God, I thought. *What am I doing here?*

But before I knew it, I was invited to sit down and I got chatting to three old dears. Me being me, I soon found myself telling them all about this accidental delivery and how the postman often made mistakes because my address was so hard to find.

Within moments I had a cup of tea in my hand and was getting to know two old men and a lovely old lady. They'd all been married and had lost their loved ones, and had little or no family.

'What's a bonnie girl like you doing on her own?' asked Bill, an 80 year old with a twinkle in his eye.

It was so easy to speak to these lovely, engaged and listening faces, and I soon found myself opening up about my disastrous love life. I told them all about Tinder and the funny dates I'd had. Before I knew it, three whole hours had passed and I hadn't laughed so much in ages.

When it was time to go, I passed Bill my number and told him to keep in touch.

Afterwards I felt so uplifted. I'd *never* have imagined I could have had such an enjoyable afternoon in an old folks' home or that such interesting, engaging people could live there.

A few weeks later I had a knock on my door and it was Bill with his carer dropping in for a visit. We had a lovely cup of tea together, catching up again. Taking time out for such unexpected company is a lovely thing to do if we're open to the idea.

For our honeymoon, Martin and I went to South Africa. But while we were there I booked us in to do a stint medical volunteering at The Zulu project, an HIV project in St Lucia, a rural village community. We helped deliver basic healthcare and lifestyle information and encouraged people to support each other in the community. We came home with so many incredible memories and it brought us even closer together, what a honeymoon!

I love a beach holiday as much as the next person, but after a few days there's only so much sun and sand you can take. To do something productive with our time is just as important and can be so enriching. That's where real memories lie, having new experiences and connecting with people who have different lives to your own. It was the first time for Martin, and I highly recommend it if you ever get the chance!

How to find your own tribe

1. **Who are you looking for?** First of all ask yourself: 'Who is missing in my life? What do I want from a tribe?' Then jot down the answers. It could be that you want more friends to have fun with, so maybe it's a new hobby you need. Or if you feel a lack of support with your work, you might need to find a supportive network in your industry. If you're not sure where to start, maybe think of what you enjoy doing already but would like to share with others. If you love reading, a local book group might be where your tribe is hiding; if you love keeping fit, sign up to a class you want to join; if you're a new mum, find a baby group for mums to chat to... the possibilities are endless. And remember, human beings are sociable creatures who need others in their lives! There will always be people like you out there.

2. **Be bold.** It's not easy finding new people to become friends with, but it is definitely possible if you try. Once you've decided you want a new tribe, the next step is finding one. Look up local meetings online, Facebook groups or notices in your library. Thanks to the Internet they will be easy to find. Then decide to take the plunge and sign up for an event or two!

3. **Commit to it.** That awkward first time is what everyone has to push through. The first or second or even third meeting might be a bit tricky, but keep going and give it a chance. Having a breakthrough will make all the awkward moments worthwhile.

4. **Stop judging.** It's easy to see someone and 'decide' whether you think you'll like them or not before they've even opened their mouths. Drop this idea and give everyone you meet a chance. Sometimes the people we think we're least likely to get along with are the ones we end up clicking with. Once my mother nagged me to meet a work colleague of hers who was several years older and I wondered what she was thinking! But after I dropped my judgement and gave this lady a chance, we actually became very close friends.

5. **Give more than you take.** Show interest in everyone else. Ask questions. Be enthusiastic. Be the first to show respect and admiration for other people's talents. People LOVE to talk about themselves and feel interesting. Chances are you will learn something and create a genuine bond.

Epilogue

Whilst I wrote this book the world was changing in ways we never thought it would. The Covid pandemic was at its peak and we all faced many ups and downs and challenges we never expected.

Lockdown was tough for a lot of us, especially for many of us small-business owners. My dental practice had completely shut down and the future was very unclear. Before the lockdown, following our wedding, I was also planning the launch of my new dental brand, Icy Bear Dental, which all came to a halt. Things were looking bleak and all of my plans had been disrupted.

How was my practice going to survive?

Was I ever going to launch my brand and make a success of it?

Covid restrictions meant filming for The Real Housewives of Cheshire was also disrupted, and although I had just started to feel more accepted in the group, it was still never plain sailing.

But like I've said, nothing is ever easy. With all the peaks came the troughs, and fitting into an established reality TV show with such big personalities was never going to be a breeze. But we made it. I learned so much and the support I've had is just incredible.

For me, writing this book has been a particular highlight. I've heard the most amazing stories from women on this journey, all while I've been articulating my own thoughts on life and how to get through it, in a way that matters to me.

I truly believe we all have potential inside of us that's often overlooked. It doesn't matter whether we think we are pretty or ugly or have big tits (or small!), we all have one thing in common and that's a brain. We all have talents we might not realise we've got at first. We all have the ability to change our habits or improve the way we think or educate ourselves to get onto the right track.

When I heard about Keira, the single mum on benefits who started her own makeup business, and Nila, the mum who didn't think she was creative while baking biscuits that were sold in Fortnum & Mason, and Carolina, who changed her direction when life got too much, and Antonina, who encouraged others to show their real selves in photographs, I was blown away.

These fabulous women proved to me what everyone is capable of, even if at first they doubt themselves.

Their stories prove that honesty, integrity and thinking outside the box can propel our lives forward in ways we could never imagine. None of the women I spoke to made their looks a priority; sure, some enjoyed fashion and makeup, but the reason why they succeeded in life was because they had one thing in common:

They used their brains.

They used their minds to think up their dreams, to overcome their challenges and ultimately to propel their lives forward. Sometimes in ways even beyond their wildest dreams.

I hope you enjoyed reading this as much as I did writing it. But most of all, I hope my story and others' will inspire your own. And if any of these rules help in any way, I'd love to hear all about it!

Love, Hanna x

Printed in Great Britain
by Amazon